THE PURSUIT OF GOD
with Study Guide

The
PURSUIT
of
GOD

WITH STUDY GUIDE
by
JONATHAN L. GRAF

A.W. TOZER

CHRISTIAN PUBLICATIONS, INC.
CAMP HILL, PENNSYLVANIA

CHRISTIAN PUBLICATIONS, INC.
3825 Hartzdale Drive, Camp Hill, PA 17011
www.christianpublications.com

Faithful, biblical publishing since 1883

ISBN: 0-87509-773-1
Pursuit of God LOC Control Number: 97-065118

The Pursuit of God Legacy Edition
© 1982, 1993 by Christian Publicatons, Inc.

The Pursuit of God Study Guide
© 1992 by Christian Publications, Inc.

02   03   04   05   06   8   7   6   5   4

Unless otherwise indicated,
Scripture taken from the
HOLY BIBLE: King James Version

The Pursuit of God and *The Pursuit of God Study Guide*
are also available separately.

Contents

FOREWORD

The Pursuit of God was the fruit of A.W. Tozer's spiritual exploration into the essence of God's nature. What resulted from the efforts of this obscure pastor from the southside of Chicago has left a profound mark on the evangelical church.

The 1949 publication of this book thrust Tozer into a respected position of spiritual leadership that he maintained for the remainder of his life. Tozer's ministry became a spiritual oasis for those of the "fellowship of the burning heart," to use a phrase he delighted in.

I was fifteen when I first discovered *The Pursuit of God*. I have read it twenty times or more. Each time I read it my soul is ministered to in a fresh way. The discovery of *The Pursuit of God* also started me on a journey into the life of this intriguing man.

Tozer's walk with God was a priority with him and he allowed nothing to interfere. It was the basis of his attraction to the Christian mystics. Their absorption in the daily practice of the presence of God was a stimulus for him and he delighted in their spiritual fellowship. He could forgive anyone almost anything if he discovered they had pure intent toward God.

Dr. Tozer's prayer life was quite remarkable. His regular habit was to sprawl on his study floor, facedown, and worship God. Often, according to his own testimony, he would lie in silent, wordless worship of God, usually oblivious to his surroundings. Such prayer and worship marked the foundation of his study and preparation for public ministry.

The desire to worship God and to inspire others to a deeper awareness of God are clearly evident in *The Pursuit of God*. For the person thirsting for the things of God without distracting embellishments, this book will become a faithful companion. There are some books that can be enjoyed with one reading, others are enhanced by many readings. *The Pursuit of God* is one of the latter.

Rev. James L. Snyder
March 1993

TOZER'S LEGACY

Quietness of soul, the fruit of truly seeking God, is seldom found in twentieth-century Christians. Far too many have come to accept turbulence of soul as the norm and have ceased to seek God with their whole hearts. Some have fled the cities to cloistered retreats in the hope of finding this quietness, only to discover their hearts still restless.

One unusual American minister who found for his own soul the secret of quietness and articulated his discovery to the Christian community was A.W. Tozer. He came upon this closer walk with God in the bustle and noise of the city of Chicago. Tozer never enjoyed the luxury of a cloistered life. Born in a poor home in the hills of western Pennsylvania, he had known hardship from as long as he could remember. Forced by his home situation to forfeit an education, Tozer entered the ministry without either high school or college training.

A.W. Tozer came to Christ at the age of seventeen, after hearing a lay preacher speaking at a street meeting in Akron, Ohio. He joined the Methodist church and became an active witness for Christ. A dingy corner of the basement of the family home became his private prayer chamber.

There, at the very beginning of his Christian life, Tozer established what was to be a lifelong practice of waiting on God.

Having become a lay preacher, Tozer found himself in disfavor with his church and decided to join with The Christian and Missionary Alliance where he found opportunity to use his gifts. His preaching ability soon made a place for him. In 1919 the district superintendent assigned Tozer to pastor the Alliance Church in Nutter Fort, West Virginia. After subsequent pastorates in Toledo and Indianapolis, he accepted a call in 1928 to Southside Alliance Church in Chicago, Illinois. His ministry in that congregation continued for thirty-one years. Avenue Road Alliance Church in Toronto, Ontario, Canada, was the last pastorate he served.

For many of the years he pastored the Chicago congregation, Tozer also preached on the Moody Bible Institute radio station WMBI. Thousands of lay people and pastors listened regularly to his rich exposition of Bible truth given on "Talks from a Pastor's Study."

His literary skills were soon recognized by his own denomination and eventually by the whole evangelical church community. In 1950 the General Council of The Christian and Missionary Alliance elected him editor of *The Alliance Witness* (now *Alliance Life*), a position he held until his death.

Aiden W. Tozer educated himself by years of diligent study and a constant prayerful seeking of the mind of God. With Tozer, seeking truth and seeking God were one and the same thing. For example, when he felt he needed an understanding of the great English works of Shakespeare, he read them through on his knees, asking God to help him understand their meaning. This procedure was typical of his method of self-education.

With no teacher but the Holy Spirit and good books, A.W. Tozer became a theologian, a scholar and a master craftsman in the use of the English language. There are not many quotes in his writings, for he had so assimilated all he had read that he could freely write in simple but attractive language the principles of truth he had discovered across these years of anointed study. The evangelical mystics were his favorite study. The longings of his own heart were satisfied by what he learned from the men and women who kept the light of spiritual reality burning in a time when apostasy and spiritual darkness seemed almost universal.

Much of the strong meat in *The Pursuit of God* came out of the crucible of Tozer's own personal experience. The chapter entitled "The Blessedness of Possessing Nothing" reflected his desperate struggle to turn his only daughter over to God. The battle for him was intense and devastating, but when full surrender came, a new and glorious release became his. He had learned to know God in the school of practical experience.

Since the first edition of *The Pursuit of God* was published in 1948, millions of copies have been printed and distributed in several languages around the world. While all of Tozer's writings are well received, *The Pursuit of God* continues to be the most popular.

The writing of this book was for A.W. Tozer a deep spiritual experience. Dr. David J. Fant, Jr., one of his biographers, describes the process:

> Tozer literally wrote *The Pursuit of God* on his knees. Perhaps that explains its power and the blessing that has rested on it.

Perhaps the continued usefulness of this book can be attributed to the writer's great spiritual discovery that to seek God does not narrow one's life, but brings it, rather, to the level of highest possible fulfillment.

A.W. Tozer was something of a twentieth- century prophet calling the modern Church back to the practice of godliness and to that level of spiritual reality enjoyed by serious seekers after God from the days of the apostles. In the legacy of his writings, none speaks more clearly to our deepest heart need than *The Pursuit of God*.

PREFACE

In this hour of all-but-universal darkness one cheering gleam appears: Within the fold of conservative Christianity there are to be found increasing numbers of persons whose religious lives are marked by a growing hunger after God Himself. They are eager for spiritual realities and will not be put off with words, nor will they be content with correct "interpretations" of truth. They are athirst for God, and they will not be satisfied till they have drunk deep at the Fountain of Living Water.

This is the only real harbinger of revival which I have been able to detect anywhere on the religious horizon. It may be the cloud the size of a man's hand for which a few saints here and there have been looking. It can result in a resurrection of life for many souls and a recapture of that radiant wonder which should accompany faith in Christ, that wonder which has all but fled the Church of God in our day.

But this hunger must be recognized by our religious leaders. Current evangelicalism has (to change the figure) laid the altar and divided the sacrifice into parts, but now seems satisfied to count the stones and rearrange the pieces with never a care that there is not a sign of fire upon the top of lofty Carmel. But God be thanked that there are a few who care. They are those who, while they love the altar and delight in the sacrifice, are yet unable to reconcile themselves to the continued absence of fire. They desire God above all. They are athirst to taste for themselves the "piercing sweetness" of the love of Christ about Whom all the holy prophets did write and the psalmists did sing.

There is today no lack of Bible teachers to set forth correctly the principles of the doctrines of Christ, but too many of these seem satisfied to teach the fundamentals of the faith year after year, strangely unaware that there is in their ministry no manifest Presence, nor anything unusual in their personal lives. They minister constantly to believers who feel within their breasts a longing which their teaching simply does not satisfy.

I trust I speak in charity, but the lack in our pulpits is real. Milton's terrible sentence applies to our day as accurately as it did to his: "The hungry sheep look up, and are not fed." It is a solemn thing, and no small scandal in the kingdom, to see God's children starving while actually seated at the Father's table. The truth of Wesley's words is established before our eyes:

> "Orthodoxy, or right opinion, is, at best, a very slender part of religion. Though right tempers cannot subsist without right opinions, yet right opinions may subsist without right tempers. There may be a right opinion

of God without either love or one right temper toward Him. Satan is a proof of this."

Thanks to our splendid Bible societies and to other effective agencies for dissemination of the Word, there are today many millions of people who hold "right opinions," probably more than ever before in the history of the Church. Yet I wonder if there was ever a time when true spiritual worship was at a lower ebb. To great sections of the Church the art of worship has been lost entirely, and in its place has come that strange and foreign thing called the "program." This word has been borrowed from the stage and applied with sad wisdom to the type of public service which now passes for worship among us.

Sound Bible exposition is an imperative *must* in the Church of the Living God. Without it no church can be a New Testament church in any strict meaning of that term. But exposition may be carried on in such a way as to leave the hearers devoid of any true spiritual nourishment whatever. For it is not mere words that nourish the soul, but God Himself, and unless and until the hearers find God in personal experience they are not the better for having heard the truth. The Bible is not an end in itself, but a means to bring men to an intimate and satisfying knowledge of God, that they may enter into Him, that they may delight in His Presence, may taste and know the inner sweetness of the very God Himself in the core and center of their hearts.

This book is a modest attempt to aid God's hungry children so to find Him. Nothing here is new except in the sense that it is a discovery which my own heart has made of spiritual realities most delightful and wonderful to me. Others before me have gone much farther into these holy mysteries than I have done, but if my fire is not large it is yet real, and there may be those who can light their candle at its flame.

A.W. Tozer
Chicago, Illinois
June 16, 1948

CHAPTER

1

Following Hard
after God

*My soul followeth hard after thee: thy right hand
upholdeth me. (Psalm 63:8)*

Christian theology teaches the doctrine of
prevenient grace, which, briefly stated,
means that before a man can seek God, God must
first have sought the man.

Before a sinful man can think a right thought of
God, there must have been a work of enlighten-
ment done within him. Imperfect it may be, but a
true work nonetheless, and the secret cause of all
desiring and seeking and praying which may follow.

We pursue God because, and only because, He
has first put an urge within us that spurs us to the
pursuit. "No man can come to me," said our Lord,
"except the Father which hath sent me draw him"

11

(John 6:44), and it is by this prevenient drawing that God takes from us every vestige of credit for the act of coming. The impulse to pursue God originates with God, but the outworking of that impulse is our following hard after Him. All the time we are pursuing Him we are already in His hand: "Thy right hand upholdeth me."

In this divine "upholding" and human "following" there is no contradiction. All is of God, for as von Hügel teaches, *God is always previous*. In practice, however, (that is, where God's previous working meets man's present response) man must pursue God. On our part there must be positive reciprocation if this secret drawing of God is to eventuate in identifiable experience of the Divine. In the warm language of personal feeling, this is stated in Psalm 42:1–2: "As the hart panteth after the water brooks, so panteth my soul after thee, O God. My soul thirsteth for God, for the living God: when shall I come and appear before God?" This is deep calling unto deep, and the longing heart will understand it.

The doctrine of justification by faith—a biblical truth, and a blessed relief from sterile legalism and unavailing self-effort—has in our time fallen into evil company and been interpreted by many in such a manner as actually to bar men from the knowledge of God. The whole transaction of religious conversion has been made mechanical and spiritless. Faith may now be exercised without a jar to the moral life and without embarrassment to the Adamic ego. Christ may be "received" without creating any special love for Him in the soul of the receiver. The man is "saved," but he is not hungry nor thirsty after God. In fact, he is specifically taught to be satisfied and is encouraged to be content with little.

The modern scientist has lost God amid the wonders of His world; we Christians are in real danger of losing God amid the wonders of His Word. We have almost forgotten that God is a person and, as such, can be cultivated as any person can. It is inherent in personality to be able to know other personalities, but full knowledge of one personality by another cannot be achieved in one encounter. It is only after long and loving mental intercourse that the full possibilities of both can be explored.

All social intercourse between human beings is a response of personality to personality, grading upward from the most casual brush between man and man to the fullest, most intimate communion of which the human soul is capable. Religion, so far as it is genuine, is in essence the response of created personalities to the creating personality, God. "This is life eternal, that they might know thee the only true God, and Jesus Christ, whom thou hast sent" (John 17:3).

God is a person, and in the deep of His mighty nature He thinks, wills, enjoys, feels, loves, desires and suffers as any other person may. In making Himself known to us He stays by the familiar pattern of personality. He communicates with us through the avenues of our minds, our wills and our emotions. The continuous and unembarrassed interchange of love and thought between God and the soul of the redeemed man is the throbbing heart of New Testament religion.

This intercourse between God and the soul is known to us in conscious personal awareness. It is personal: it does not come through the body of believers, as such, but is known to the individual, and to the body through the individuals which compose it. It is conscious: it does not stay below the threshold of consciousness and work there unknown to the soul (as, for instance, infant baptism is thought by some to do), but comes within the field of awareness where the man can know it as he knows any other fact of experience.

You and I are in little (our sins excepted) what God is in large. Being made in His image we have within us the capacity to know Him. In our sins we lack only the power. The moment the Spirit has quickened us to life in regeneration our whole being senses its kinship to God and leaps up in joyous recognition. That is the heavenly birth without which we cannot see the kingdom of God. It is, however, not an end but an inception, for now begins the glorious pursuit, the heart's happy exploration of the infinite riches of the Godhead. That is where we begin, I say, but where we stop no man has yet discovered, for there is in the awful and mysterious depths of the Triune God neither limit nor end.

> Shoreless Ocean, who can sound
>   Thee?

> Thine own eternity is round Thee,
>   Majesty divine!

To have found God and still to pursue Him is the soul's paradox of love, scorned indeed by the too easily satisfied religionist, but justified in happy experience by the children of the burning heart. St. Bernard stated this holy paradox in a musical quatrain that will be instantly understood by every worshiping soul:

> We taste Thee, O Thou Living Bread,
>   And long to feast upon Thee still:
> We drink of Thee, the Fountainhead
>   And thirst our souls from Thee to
>   fill.

Come near to the holy men and women of the past and you will soon feel the heat of their desire after God. They mourned for Him, they prayed and wrestled and sought for Him day and night, in season and out, and when they had found Him the finding was all the sweeter for the long seeking. Moses used the fact that he knew God as an argument for knowing Him better. "Now therefore, I pray thee, if I have found grace in thy sight, shew me now thy way, that I may know thee, that I may find grace in thy sight" (Exodus 33:13); and from there he rose to make the daring request, "I beseech thee, shew me thy glory" (33:18). God was frankly pleased by this display of ardor, and the next day called Moses into the mount, and there in solemn procession made all His glory pass before him.

David's life was a torrent of spiritual desire, and his psalms ring with the cry of the seeker and the glad shout of the finder. Paul confessed the mainspring of his life to be his burning desire after Christ. "That I may know him" (Philippians 3:10), was the goal of his heart, and to this he sacrificed everything. "Yea doubtless, and I count all things but loss for the excellency of the knowledge of Christ Jesus my Lord: for whom I have suffered the loss of all things, and do count them but dung, that I may win Christ" (3:8).

Hymnody is sweet with the longing after God, the God whom, while the singer seeks, he knows he has already found. "His track I see and I'll pursue," sang our fathers only a short generation ago, but that song is heard no more in the great congregation. How tragic that we in this dark day have had our seeking done for us by our teachers. Everything is made to center upon the initial act of "accepting" Christ (a term, incidentally, which is not found in the Bible) and we are not expected thereafter to crave any further revelation of God to our souls. We have been snared in the coils of a spurious logic which insists that if we have found Him, we need no more seek Him. This is set before us as the last word in orthodoxy, and it is taken for granted that no Bible-taught Christian ever believed otherwise. Thus the whole testimony of the worshiping, seeking, singing church on that subject is crisply set aside. The experiential heart-theology of a grand army of fragrant saints is rejected in favor of a smug interpretation of Scripture which would certainly have sounded strange to an Augustine, a Rutherford or a Brainerd.

In the midst of this great chill there are some, I rejoice to acknowledge, who will not be content with shallow logic. They will admit the force of the argument, and then turn away with tears to hunt some lonely place and pray, "O God, show me Thy glory." They want to taste, to touch with their hearts, to see with their inner eyes the wonder that is God.

I want deliberately to encourage this mighty longing after God. The lack of it has brought us to our present low estate. The stiff and wooden quality about our religious lives is a result of our lack of holy desire. Complacency is a deadly foe of all spiritual growth. Acute desire must be present or there will be no manifestation of Christ to His people. He waits to be wanted. Too bad that with many of us He waits so long, so very long, in vain.

Every age has its own characteristics. Right now we are in an age of religious complexity. The simplicity which is in Christ is rarely found among us. In its stead are programs, methods, organizations and a world of nervous activities which occupy time and attention but can never satisfy the longing of the heart. The shallowness of our inner experience, the hollowness of our worship and that servile imitation of the world which marks our promotional methods all testify that we, in this day, know God only imperfectly, and the peace of God scarcely at all.

If we would find God amid all the religious externals, we must first determine to find Him, and then proceed in the way of simplicity. Now, as always, God discovers Himself to "babes" and hides Himself in thick darkness from the wise and the prudent. We must simplify our approach to Him. We must strip down to essentials (and they will be found to be blessedly few). We must put away all effort to impress, and come with the guileless candor of childhood. If we do this, without doubt God will quickly respond.

When religion has said its last word, there is little that we need other than God Himself. The evil habit of seeking *God-and* effectively prevents us from finding God in full revelation. In the *and* lies our great woe. If we omit the *and* we shall soon find God, and in Him we shall find that for which we have all our lives been secretly longing.

We need not fear that in seeking God only we may narrow our lives or restrict the motions of our expanding hearts. The opposite is true. We can well afford to make God our All, to concentrate, to sacrifice the many for the One.

The author of the quaint old English classic, *The Cloud of Unknowing*, teaches us how to do this.

> "Lift up thine heart unto God with a meek stirring of love; and mean Himself, and none of His goods. And thereto, look thee loath to think on aught but God Himself. So that nought work in thy wit, nor in thy will, but only God Himself. This is the work of the soul that most pleaseth God."

Again, he recommends that in prayer we practice a further stripping down of everything, even of our theology. "For it sufficeth enough, a naked intent direct unto God without any other cause than Himself." Yet underneath all his thinking lay the broad foundation of New Testament truth, for he explains that by "Himself" he means "God that made thee, and bought thee, and that graciously called thee, to thy degree." And he is all for simplicity: If we would have religion "lapped and folden in one word, for that thou shouldest have better hold thereupon, take thee but a little word of one syllable: for so it is better than of two, for even the shorter it is the better it accordeth with the work of the Spirit. And such a word is this word GOD or this word LOVE."

When the Lord divided Canaan among the tribes of Israel, Levi received no share of the land. God said to him simply, "I am thy part and thine inheritance," and by those words made him richer than all his brethren, richer than all the kings and rajas who have ever lived in the world. And there is a spiritual principle here, a principle still valid for every priest of the Most High God.

The man who has God for his treasure has all things in One. Many ordinary treasures may be denied him, or if he is allowed to have them, the enjoyment of them will be so tempered that they will never be necessary to his happiness. Or if he must see them go, one after one, he will scarcely feel a sense of loss, for having the Source of all things he has in One all satisfaction, all pleasure, all delight. Whatever he may lose he has actually lost nothing, for he now has it all in One, and he has it purely, legitimately and forever.

*   *   *

O God, I have tasted Thy goodness, and it has both satisfied me and made me thirsty for more. I am painfully conscious of my need of further grace. I am ashamed of my lack of desire. O God, the Triune God, I want to want Thee; I long to be filled with longing; I thirst to be made more thirsty still. Show me Thy glory, I pray Thee, that so I may know Thee indeed. Begin in mercy a new work of love within me. Say to my soul, "Rise up, my love, my fair one, and come away." Then give me grace to rise and follow Thee up from this misty lowland where I have wandered so long.
In Jesus' name.
Amen.

The Blessedness of Possessing Nothing

Blessed are the poor in spirit: for theirs is the kingdom of heaven. (Matthew 5:3)

Before the Lord God made man upon the earth He first prepared for him a world of useful and pleasant things for his sustenance and delight. In the Genesis account of the creation these are simply "things." They were made for man's use, but they were meant always to be external to the man and subservient to him. In the deep heart of the man was a shrine where none but God was worthy to come. Within him was God; without, a thousand gifts which God had showered upon him.

But sin has introduced complications and has made those very gifts of God a potential source of ruin to the soul.

Our woes began when God was forced out of His central shrine and things were allowed to enter. Within the human heart things have taken over. Men have now by nature no peace within their hearts, for God is crowned there no longer, but there in the moral dusk, stubborn and aggressive usurpers fight among themselves for first place on the throne.

This is not a mere metaphor, but an accurate analysis of our real spiritual trouble. There is within the human heart a tough, fibrous root of fallen life whose nature is to possess, always to possess. It covets things with a deep and fierce passion. The pronouns *my* and *mine* look innocent enough in print, but their constant and universal use is significant. They express the real nature of the old Adamic man better than a thousand volumes of theology could do. They are verbal symptoms of our deep disease. The roots of our hearts have grown down into things, and we dare not pull up one rootlet lest we die. Things have become necessary to us, a development never originally intended. God's gifts now take the place of God, and the whole course of nature is upset by the monstrous substitution.

Our Lord referred to this tyranny of things when He said to His disciples,

> If any man will come after me, let him deny himself, and take up his cross, and follow me. For whosoever will save his life shall lose it: and whosoever will lose his life for my sake shall find it. (Matthew 16:24–25)

Breaking this truth into fragments for our better understanding, it would seem that there is within each of us an enemy which we tolerate at our peril. Jesus called it "life" and "self," or as we would say, the *self-life*. Its chief characteristic is its possessiveness; the words *gain* and *profit* suggest this. To allow this enemy to live is, in the end, to lose everything. To repudiate it and give up all for Christ's sake is to lose nothing at last, but to preserve everything unto life eternal. And possibly also a hint is given here as to the only effective way to destroy this foe: It is by the cross. "Let him take up his cross, and follow me" (see Matthew 16:24).

The way to deeper knowledge of God is through the lonely valleys of soul poverty and abnegation of all things. The blessed ones who possess the kingdom are they who have repudiated every external thing and have rooted from their hearts all sense of possessing. These are the "poor in spirit." They have reached an inward state paralleling the outward circumstances of the common beggar in the streets of Jerusalem. That is what the word *poor* as Christ used it actually means. These blessed poor are no longer slaves to the tyranny of things. They have broken the yoke of the oppressor; and this they have done not by fighting but by surrendering. Though free from all sense of possessing, they yet possess all things. "Theirs is the kingdom of heaven."

Let me exhort you to take this seriously. It is not to be understood as mere Bible teaching to be stored away in the mind along with an inert mass of other doctrines. It is a marker on the road to greener pastures, a path chiseled against the steep sides of the mount of God. We dare not try to bypass it if we would follow on in this holy pursuit. We must ascend a step at a time. If we refuse one step, we bring our progress to an end.

As is frequently true, this New Testament principle of spiritual life finds its best illustration in the Old Testament. In the story of Abraham and Isaac we have a dramatic picture of the surrendered life as well as an excellent commentary on the first Beatitude.

Abraham was old when Isaac was born, old enough to have been his grandfather, and the child became at once the delight and idol of his heart. From the moment he first stooped to take the tiny form awkwardly in his arms, he was an eager love slave of his son. God went out of His way to comment on the strength of this affection. And it is not hard to understand. The baby represented everything sacred to his father's heart: the promises of God, the covenants, the hopes of the years and the long messianic dream. As he watched him grow from babyhood to young manhood, the heart of the old man was knit closer and closer with the life of his son, till at last the relationship bordered upon the perilous. It was then that God stepped in to save both father and son from the consequences of an uncleansed love.

"Take now thy son," said God to Abraham, "thine only son Isaac, whom thou lovest, and get thee into the land of Moriah; and offer him there for a burnt offering upon one of the mountains which I will tell thee of" (Genesis 22:2). The sacred writer spares us a close-up of the agony that night on the slopes near Beersheba when the aged man had it out with his God, but respectful imagination may view in awe the bent form wrestling convulsively alone under the stars. Possibly not again until One greater than Abraham wrestled in the Garden of Gethsemane did such mortal pain visit a human soul. If only the man himself might have been allowed to die. That would have been a thousand times easier, for he was old now, and to die would have been no great ordeal for one who had walked so long with God. Besides, it would have been a last, sweet pleasure to let his dimming vision rest upon the figure of his stalwart son who would live to carry on the Abrahamic line and fulfill in himself the promises of God made long before in Ur of the Chaldees.

How should he slay the lad! Even if he could get the consent of his wounded and protesting heart, how could he reconcile the act with the promise, "In Isaac shall thy seed be called"? This was Abraham's trial by fire, and he did not fail in the crucible. While the stars still shone like sharp white points above the tent where the sleeping Isaac lay, and long before the gray dawn had begun to lighten the east, the old saint had made up his mind. He would offer his son as God had directed him to do, and then *trust God to raise him from the dead*. This, says the writer to the Hebrews, was the solution his aching heart found sometime in the dark night, and he rose "early in the morning" to carry out the plan. It is beautiful to see that, while he erred as to God's method, he had correctly sensed the secret of His great heart. And the solution accords well with the New Testament Scripture, "Whosoever will lose . . . for my sake shall find" (Matthew 16:25).

God let the suffering old man go through with it up to the point where He knew there would be no retreat, and then forbade him to lay a hand upon the boy. To the wondering patriarch He now says in effect, "It's all right, Abraham. I never intended that you should actually slay the lad. I only wanted to remove him from the temple of your heart that I might reign unchallenged there. I wanted to correct the perversion that existed in your love. Now you may have the boy, sound and well. Take him and go back to your tent. Now I know that thou fearest God, seeing that thou hast not withheld thy son, thine only son, from Me."

Then heaven opened and a voice was heard saying to him,

> "By myself have I sworn, saith the LORD, for because thou hast done this thing, and hast not withheld thy son, thine only son: that in blessing I will bless thee, and in multiplying I will multiply thy seed as the stars of the heaven, and as the sand which is upon the sea shore; and thy seed shall possess the gate of his enemies; and in thy seed shall all the nations of the earth be blessed; because thou hast obeyed my voice" (Genesis 22:16–18).

The old man of God lifted his head to respond to the Voice, and stood there on the mount strong and pure and grand, a man marked out by the Lord for special treatment, a friend and favorite of the Most High. Now he was a man wholly surrendered, a man utterly obedient, a man who possessed nothing. He had concentrated his all in the person of his dear son and God had taken it from him. God could have begun out on the margin of Abraham's life and worked inward to the center. He chose rather to cut quickly to the heart and have it over in one sharp act of separation. In dealing thus, He practiced an economy of means and time. It hurt cruelly, but it was effective.

I have said that Abraham possessed nothing. Yet was not this poor man rich? Everything he had owned before was his still to enjoy: sheep, camels, herds and goods of every sort. He had also his wife and his friends, and best of all he had his son Isaac safe by his side. He had everything, *but he possessed nothing*. There is the spiritual secret. There is the sweet theology of the heart which can be learned only in the school of renunciation. The books on systematic theology overlook this, but the wise will understand.

After that bitter and blessed experience I think the words *my* and *mine* never again had the same meaning for Abraham. The sense of possession which they connote was gone from his heart. Things had been cast out forever. They had now become external to the man. His inner heart was free from them. The world said, "Abraham is rich," but the aged patriarch only smiled. He could not explain it, but he knew that he owned nothing, that his real treasures were inward and eternal.

There can be no doubt that this possessive clinging to things is one of the most harmful habits in the life. Because it is natural, it is rarely recognized for the evil that it is. But its outworkings are tragic.

We are often hindered from giving up our treasures to the Lord out of fear for their safety. This is especially true when those treasures are loved relatives and friends. But we need have no such fears. Our Lord came not to destroy but to save. Everything is safe which we commit to Him, and nothing is really safe which is not so committed.

Our gifts and talents should also be turned over to Him. They should be recognized for what they are, God's loan to us, and should never be considered in any sense our own. We have no more right to claim credit for special abilities than for blue eyes or strong muscles. "For who maketh thee to differ from another? and what hast thou that thou didst not receive?" (1 Corinthians 4:7).

The Christian who is alive enough to know himself even slightly will recognize the symptoms of this possession malady, and will grieve to find them in his own heart. If the longing after God is strong enough within him, he will want to do something about the matter. Now, what should he do?

First of all, he should put away all defense and make no attempt to excuse himself either in his own eyes or before the Lord. Whoever defends himself will have himself for his defense, and he will have no other. But let him come defenseless before the Lord and he will have for his defender no less than God

Himself. Let the inquiring Christian trample under foot every slippery trick of his deceitful heart and insist upon frank and open relations with the Lord.

Then he should remember that this is holy business. No careless or casual dealings will suffice. Let him come to God fully determined to be heard. Let him insist that God accept his all, that He take things out of his heart and Himself reign there in power. It may be he will need to become specific, to name things and people by their names one by one. If he will become drastic enough, he can shorten the time of his travail from years to minutes and enter the good land long before his slower brethren who coddle their feelings and insist upon caution in their dealing with God.

Let us never forget that a truth such as this cannot be learned by rote as one would learn the facts of physical science. They must be *experienced* before we can really know them. We must, in our hearts, live through Abraham's harsh and bitter experiences if we would know the blessedness which follows them. The ancient curse will not go out painlessly; the tough old miser within us will not lie down and die in obedience to our command. He must be torn out of our heart like a plant from the soil; he must be extracted in agony and blood like a tooth from the jaw. He must be expelled from our soul by violence, as Christ expelled the money changers from the temple. And we shall need to steel ourselves against his piteous begging, and to recognize it as springing out of self-pity, one of the most reprehensible sins of the human heart.

If we would indeed know God in growing intimacy, we must go this way of renunciation. And if we are set upon the pursuit of God, He will sooner or later bring us to this test. Abraham's testing was, at the time, not known to him as such, yet if he had taken some course other than the one he did, the whole history of the Old Testament would have been different. God would have found his man, no doubt, but the loss to Abraham would have been tragic beyond the telling. So we will be brought one by one to the testing place, and we may never know when we are there. At that testing place there will be no dozen possible choices for us—just one and an alternative—but our whole future will be conditioned by the choice we make.

*   *   *

Father, I want to know Thee, but my cowardly heart fears to give up its toys. I cannot part with them without inward bleeding, and I do not try to hide from Thee the terror of the parting. I come trembling, but I do come. Please root from my heart all those things which I have cherished so long and which have become a very part of my living self, so that Thou mayest enter and dwell there without a rival. Then shalt Thou make the place of Thy feet glorious. Then shall my heart have no need of the sun to shine in it, for Thyself wilt be the light of it, and there shall be no night there.
In Jesus' name.
Amen.

Removing the Veil

Having therefore, brethren, boldness to enter into the holiest by the blood of Jesus. (Hebrews 10:19)

Among the famous sayings of the church fathers, none is better known than Augustine's, "Thou hast formed us for Thyself, and our hearts are restless till they find rest in Thee."

The great saint states here in few words the origin and interior history of the human race. God made us for Himself—this is the only explanation that satisfies the heart of a thinking man, whatever his wild reason may say. Should faulty education and perverse reasoning lead a man to conclude otherwise, there is little that any Christian can do for him. For such a man I have no message. My appeal is addressed to those who have been previously taught in secret by the wisdom of God. I speak to thirsty hearts whose longings have been wakened by the touch of God within them, and such as they need no reasoned proof. Their restless hearts furnish all the proof they need.

God formed us for Himself. *The Shorter Catechism*, "Agreed upon by the Reverend Assembly of Divines at Westminster," as the old *New England Primer* has it, asks the ancient questions *what* and *why* and answers them in one short sentence hardly matched in any uninspired work. "*Question*: What is the chief end of man? *Answer:* Man's chief end is to glorify God and enjoy Him forever." With this agree the four and twenty elders who fall on their faces to worship Him that liveth forever and ever, saying, "Thou art worthy, O Lord, to receive glory and honour and power: for thou hast created all things, and for thy pleasure they are and were created" (Revelation 4:11).

Ephesians 1:12

God formed us for His pleasure, and so formed us that we, as well as He, can, in divine communion, enjoy the sweet and mysterious mingling of kindred personalities. He meant us to see Him and live with Him and draw our life from His smile. But we have been guilty of that "foul revolt" of which Milton speaks when describing the rebellion of Satan and his hosts. We have broken with God. We have ceased to obey Him or love Him, and in guilt and fear have fled as far as possible from His presence.

Yet, who can flee from His presence when the heaven and the heaven of heavens cannot contain Him? when as the wisdom of Solomon testifies, "the Spirit of the Lord filleth the world"? The omnipresence of the Lord is one thing and is a solemn fact necessary to His perfection. The manifest Presence is another thing altogether, and from that Presence we have fled, like Adam, to hide among the trees of the garden, or like Peter, to shrink away crying, "Depart from me; for I am a sinful man, O Lord" (Luke 5:8).

So the life of man upon the earth is a life away from the Presence, wrenched loose from that "blissful center" which is our right and proper dwelling place, our first estate which we kept not, the loss of which is the cause of our unceasing restlessness.

The whole work of God in redemption is to undo the tragic effects of that foul revolt, and to bring us back again into right and eternal relationship with Himself. This requires that our sins be disposed of satisfactorily, that a full reconciliation be effected and the way opened for us to return again into conscious communion with God and to live again in the Presence as before. Then by His prevenient working within us He moves us to return. This first comes to our notice when our restless hearts feel a yearning for the presence of God and we say within ourselves, "I will arise and go to my Father." That is the first step, and as the Chinese sage Lao-tze has said, "The journey of a thousand miles begins with a first step."

The interior journey of the soul from the wilds of sin into the enjoyed presence of God is beautifully illustrated in the Old Testament tabernacle. The returning sinner first entered the outer court where he offered a blood sacrifice on the brazen altar and washed himself in the laver that stood near it. Then he passed through a veil into the holy place where no natural light could come, but the golden candlestick which spoke of Jesus, the Light of the World, threw its soft glow over all. There also was the shewbread to tell of Jesus, the Bread of Life, and the altar of incense, a figure of unceasing prayer.

Though the worshiper had enjoyed so much, still he had not yet entered the presence of God. Another veil separated from the Holy of Holies where above the mercy seat dwelt the very God Himself in awful and glorious manifestation. While the tabernacle stood, only the high priest could enter there, and that but once a year, with blood which he offered for his sins and the sins of the people. It was this last veil which was rent when our Lord gave up the ghost on Calvary, and the sacred writer explains that this rending of the veil opened the way for every worshiper in the world to come by the new and living way straight into the divine Presence.

Everything in the New Testament accords with this Old Testament picture. Ransomed men need no longer pause in fear to enter the Holy of Holies. *God wills that we should push on into His presence and live our whole life there.* This is to be known to us in conscious experience. It is more than a doctrine to be held; it is a life to be enjoyed every moment of every day.

This Flame of the Presence was the beating heart of the Levitical order. Without it all the appointments of the tabernacle were characters of some unknown language, having no meaning for Israel or for us. The greatest fact of the tabernacle was that *Jehovah was there*; a Presence was waiting within the veil.

Similarly, the presence of God is the central fact of Christianity. At the heart of the Christian message is God Himself waiting for His redeemed children to push in to conscious awareness of His presence. That type of Christianity which happens now to be the vogue knows this Presence only in theory. It fails to stress the Christian's privilege of present realization. According to its teachings we are in the presence of God positionally, and nothing is said about the need to experience that Presence actually. The fiery urge that drove men like McCheyne is wholly missing. And the present generation of Christians measures itself by this imperfect rule. Ignoble contentment takes the place of burning zeal. We are satisfied to rest in our judicial possessions and, for the most part, we bother ourselves very little about the absence of personal experience.

Who is this within the veil who dwells in fiery manifestations? It is none other than God Himself.

"One God, the Father Almighty, Maker of heaven and earth, and of all things visible and invisible." It is "one Lord Jesus Christ, the only begotten Son of God; begotten of His Father before all worlds, God of God, Light of Light, Very God of Very God; begotten, not made; being of one substance with the Father."

And it is "the Holy Ghost, the Lord and Giver of life, Who proceedeth from the Father and the Son,

Who with the Father and the Son together is worshiped and glorified." Yet this holy Trinity is one God, for

> "we worship one God in Trinity, and Trinity in Unity; neither confounding the Persons, nor dividing the Substance. For there is one Person of the Father, another of the Son, and another of the Holy Ghost. But the Godhead of the Father, of the Son, and of the Holy Ghost, is all one: the glory equal and the majesty co-eternal."

So in part run the ancient creeds, and so the inspired Word declares.

Behind the veil is God, that God after whom the world, with strange inconsistency, has felt, "if haply they might . . . find him" (Acts 17:27). He has discovered Himself to some extent in nature, but more perfectly in the Incarnation. Now He waits to show Himself in ravishing fullness to the humble of soul and the pure in heart.

The world is perishing for lack of the knowledge of God and the Church is famishing for want of His presence. The instant cure of most of our religious ills would be to enter the Presence in spiritual experience, to become suddenly aware that we are in God and God is in us. This would lift us out of our pitiful narrowness and cause our hearts to be enlarged. This would burn away the impurities from our lives as the bugs and fungi were burned away by the fire that dwelt in the bush.

What a broad world to roam in, what a sea to swim in is this God and Father of our Lord Jesus Christ. He is *eternal*. He antedates time and is wholly independent of it. Time began in Him and will end in Him. To it He pays no tribute and from it He suffers no change.

He is *immutable*. He has never changed and can never change in any smallest measure. To change He would need to go from better to worse or from worse to better. He cannot do either, for being perfect He cannot become more perfect, and if He were to become less perfect He would be less than God.

He is *omniscient*. He knows in one free and effortless act all matter, all spirit, all relationships, all events. He has no past and He has no future. He *is*, and none of the limiting and qualifying terms used of creatures can apply to Him.

Love and mercy and righteousness are His, and *holiness* so ineffable that no comparisons or figures will avail to express it. Only fire can give even a remote conception of it. In fire He appeared at the burning bush; in the pillar of fire He dwelt through all the long wilderness journey. The fire that glowed between the wings of the cherubim in the holy place was called the Shekinah, the Presence, through the years of Israel's glory, and when the Old had given place to the New, He came at Pentecost as a fiery flame and rested upon each disciple.

Spinoza wrote of the intellectual love of God, and he had a measure of truth there. But the highest love of God is not intellectual, it is spiritual. God is Spirit and only the spirit of a man can know Him really. In the deep spirit of a man the fire must glow or his love is not the true love of God. The great of the kingdom have been those who loved God more than others did. We all know who they have been and gladly pay tribute to the depth and sincerity of their devotion. We have but to pause for a moment and their names come trooping past us, smelling of myrrh and aloes and cassia out of the ivory palaces.

Frederick Faber was one whose soul panted after God as the roe deer pants after the water brook, and the measure in which God revealed Himself to his seeking heart set the good man's whole life afire with a burning adoration rivaling that of the seraphim before the throne. His love for God extended to the three Persons of the Godhead equally, yet he seemed to feel for each One a special kind of love reserved for Him alone. Of God the Father he sings:

> Only to sit and think of God
> Oh what a joy it is!
> To think the thought, to breathe the
> Name;
> Earth has no higher bliss.
> Father of Jesus, love's reward!
> What rapture it will be,
> Prostrate before Thy throne to lie,
> And gaze and gaze on Thee!

His love for the Person of Christ was so intense that it threatened to consume him. It burned within him as a sweet and holy madness and flowed from his lips like molten gold. In one of his sermons he says,

Wherever we turn in the church of God, there is Jesus. He is the beginning, middle and end of everything to us. . . . There is nothing good, nothing holy, nothing beautiful, nothing joyous which He is not to His servants. No one need to be poor, because, if he chooses, he can have Jesus for his own property and possession. No one need be downcast, for Jesus is the joy of heaven, and it is His joy to enter into sorrowful hearts. We can exaggerate about many things; but we can never exaggerate our obligation to Jesus or the compassionate abundance of the love of Jesus to us. All our lives long we might talk of Jesus, and yet we should never come to an end of the sweet things that might be said of Him. Eternity will not be long enough to learn all He is, or to praise Him for all He has done, but then, that matters not; for we shall be always with Him, and we desire nothing more.

And addressing our Lord directly he says to Him:

I love Thee so, I know not how
    My transports to control;
Thy love is like a burning fire
    Within my very soul.

Faber's blazing love extended also to the Holy Spirit. Not only in his theology did he acknowledge His deity and full equality with the Father and the Son, but he celebrated it constantly in his songs and in his prayers. He literally pressed his forehead to the ground in his eager, fervid worship of the Third Person of the Godhead. In one of his great hymns to the Holy Spirit he sums up his burning devotion thus:

> O Spirit, beautiful and dread!
>   My heart is fit to break
> With love of all Thy tenderness
>   For us poor sinners' sake.

I have risked the tedium of quotation that I might show by pointed example what I have set out to say, viz., that God is so vastly wonderful, so utterly and completely delightful that He can, without anything other than Himself, meet and overflow the deepest demands of our total nature, mysterious and deep as that nature is. Such worship as Faber knew (and he is but one of a great company which no man can number) can never come from a mere doctrinal knowledge of God. Hearts that are "fit to break" with love for the Godhead are those who have been in the Presence and have looked with opened eye upon the majesty of Deity. Men of the breaking hearts had a quality about them not known to nor understood by common men. They habitually spoke with spiritual authority. They had been in the presence of God and they reported what they saw there.

They were prophets, not scribes, for the scribe tells us what he has read, and the prophet tells what he has seen. The distinction is not an imaginary one. Between the scribe who has read and the prophet who has seen there is a difference as wide as the sea. We are overrun today with orthodox scribes, but the prophets, where are they? The hard voice of the scribe sounds over evangelicalism, but the church waits for the tender voice of the saint who has penetrated the veil and has gazed with inward eye upon the wonder that is God. And yet, thus to penetrate, to push in sensitive living experience into the holy Presence, is a privilege open to every child of God.

With the veil removed by the rending of Jesus' flesh, with nothing on God's side to prevent us from entering, why do we tarry without? Why do we consent to abide all our days just outside the Holy of Holies and never enter at all to look upon God? We hear the Bridegroom say, "Let me see thy countenance, let me hear thy voice; for sweet is thy voice, and thy countenance is comely" (Song of Solomon 2:14). We sense that the call is for us, but still we fail to draw near, and the years pass and we grow old and tired in the outer courts of the tabernacle. What hinders us?

The answer usually given, simply that we are "cold," will not explain all the facts. There is something more serious than coldness of heart, something that may be back of that coldness and be the cause of its existence. What is it? What but the presence of a *veil in our hearts*? A veil not taken away as the first veil was, but which remains there still shutting out the light and hiding the face of God from us. It is the veil of our fleshly, fallen nature living on, unjudged within us, uncrucified and unrepu- diated. It is the close-woven veil of the self-life which we have never truly acknowledged, of which we have been secretly ashamed, and which for these reasons we have never brought to the judgment of the cross. It is not too mysterious, this opaque veil, nor is it hard to identify. We have but to look into our own hearts and we shall see it there, sewn and patched and repaired it may be, but there nevertheless, an enemy to our lives and an effective block to our spiritual progress.

This veil is not a beautiful thing and it is not a thing about which we commonly care to talk. But I am addressing the thirsting souls who are determined to follow God, and I know they will not turn back because the way leads temporarily through the blackened hills. The urge of God within them will assure their continuing pursuit. They will face the facts however unpleasant and endure the cross for the joy set before them. So I am bold to name the threads out of which this inner veil is woven.

It is woven of the fine threads of the self-life, the hyphenated sins of the human spirit. They are not something we *do*, they are something we *are*, and therein lies both their subtlety and their power.

To be specific, the self-sins are self-righteousness, self-pity, self-confidence, self- sufficiency, self-admiration, self-love and a host of others like them. They dwell too deep within us and are too much a part of our natures to come to our attention till the light of God is focused upon them. The grosser manifestations of these sins—egotism, exhibitionism, self-promotion—are strangely tolerated in Christian leaders, even in circles of impeccable orthodoxy. They are so much in evidence as actually, for many people, to become identified with the gospel. I trust it is not a cynical observation to say that they appear these days to be a requisite for popularity in some sections of the church visible. Promoting self under the guise of promoting Christ is currently so common as to excite little notice.

One should suppose that proper instruction in the doctrines of man's depravity and the necessity for justification through the righteousness of Christ alone would deliver us from the power of the self-sins, but it does not work that way. Self can live unrebuked at the very altar. It can watch the bleeding Victim die and not be in the least affected by what it sees. It can fight for the faith of the reformers and preach eloquently the creed of salvation by grace and gain strength by its efforts. To tell the truth, it seems actually to feed upon orthodoxy and is more at home in a Bible conference than in a tavern. Our very state of longing after God may afford it an excellent condition under which to thrive and grow.

Self is the opaque veil that hides the face of God from us. It can be removed only in spiritual experience, never by mere instruction. We may as well try to instruct leprosy out of our system. There must be a work of God in destruction before we are free. We must invite the cross to do its deadly work within us. We must bring our self-sins to the cross for judgment. We must prepare ourselves for an ordeal of suffering in some measure like that through which our Savior passed when He suffered under Pontius Pilate.

Let us remember that when we talk of the rending of the veil we are speaking in a figure, and the thought of it is poetical, almost pleasant, but in actuality there is nothing pleasant about it. In human experience that veil is made of living spiritual tissue; it is composed of the sentient, quivering stuff of which our whole beings consist, and to touch it is to touch us where we feel pain. To tear it away is to injure us, to hurt us and make us bleed. To say otherwise is to make the cross no cross and death no death at all. It is never fun to die. To rip through the dear and tender stuff of which life is made can never be anything but deeply painful. Yet that is what the cross did to Jesus and it is what the cross would do to every man to set him free.

Let us beware of tinkering with our inner life, hoping ourselves to rend the veil. God must do everything for us. Our part is to yield and trust. We must confess, forsake, repudiate the self-life, and then reckon it crucified. But we must be careful to distinguish lazy "acceptance" from the real work of God. We must insist upon the work being done. We dare not rest content with a neat doctrine of self-crucifixion. That is to imitate Saul and spare the best of the sheep and the oxen.

Insist that the work be done in very truth and it will be done. The cross is rough and it is deadly, but it is effective. It does not keep its victim hanging there forever. There comes a moment when its work is finished and the suffering victim dies. After that is resurrection glory and power, and the pain is forgotten for joy that the veil is taken away and we have entered in actual spiritual experience the presence of the living God.

*   *   *

Lord, how excellent are Thy ways, and how devious and dark are the ways of man. Show us how to die, that we may rise again to newness of life. Rend the veil of our self-life from the top down as Thou didst rend the veil of the Temple. We would draw near in full assurance of faith. We would dwell with Thee in daily experience here on this earth so that we may be accustomed to the glory when we enter Thy heaven to dwell with Thee there.
In Jesus' name.
Amen.

Apprehending God

O taste and see. (Psalm 34:8)

anon Holmes, of India, more than twenty-five years ago called attention to the inferential character of the average man's faith in God. To most people God is an inference, not a reality. He is a deduction from evidence which they consider adequate, but He remains personally unknown to the individual. "He *must* be," they say, "therefore we believe He is." Others do not go even so far as this; they know of Him only by hearsay. They have never bothered to think the matter out for themselves, but have heard about Him from others, and have put belief in Him into the back of their minds along with various odds and ends that make up their total creed. To many others, God is but an ideal, another name for goodness or beauty or truth; or He is law or life or the creative impulse back of the phenomena of existence.

These notions about God are many and varied, but they who hold them have one thing in common: They do not know God in personal experience. The possibility of intimate acquaintance with Him has not entered their minds. While admitting His existence they do not think of Him as being knowable in the sense that we know things or people.

Christians, to be sure, go further than this, at least in theory. Their creed requires them to believe in the personality of God and they have been taught to pray, "Our Father which art in heaven" (Luke 11:2). Now personality and fatherhood carry with them the idea of the possibility of personal acquaintance. This is admitted, I say, in theory, but for millions of Christians, nevertheless, God is no more real than He is to the non-Christian. They go through life trying to love an ideal and be loyal to a mere principle.

Over against all this cloudy vagueness stands the clear scriptural doctrine that God can be known in personal experience. A loving Personality dominates the Bible, walking among the trees of the garden and breathing fragrance over every scene. Always a living Person is present, speaking, pleading, loving, working and manifesting Himself whenever and wherever His people have the receptivity necessary to receive the manifestation.

The Bible assumes as a self-evident fact that men can know God with at least the same degree of immediacy as they know any other person or thing that comes within the field of their experience. The same terms are used to express the knowledge of God as are used to express knowledge of physical things. "O *taste* and *see* that the LORD is good" (Psalm 34:8, emphasis added). "All thy garments *smell* of myrrh, and aloes, and cassia, out of the ivory palaces" (45:8). "My sheep *hear* my voice" (John 10:27, emphasis added). "Blessed are the pure in heart: for they shall *see* God" (Matthew 5:8, emphasis added). These are but four of countless such passages from the Word of God. And more important than any proof text is the fact that the whole import of Scripture is toward this belief.

What can all this mean except that we have in our hearts organs by means of which we can know God as certainly as we know material things through our familiar five senses? We apprehend the physical world by exercising the faculties given us for that purpose, and we possess spiritual faculties by means of which we can know God and the spiritual world if we will obey the Spirit's urge and begin to use them.

That a saving work must first be done in the heart is taken for granted here. The spiritual faculties of the unregenerate man lie asleep in his nature, unused, and for every purpose dead. That is the stroke which has fallen upon us by sin. They may be quickened to active life again by the operation of the Holy Spirit in regeneration. That is one of the immeasurable benefits which comes to us through Christ's atoning work on the cross.

But why do the very ransomed children of God themselves know so little of that habitual, conscious communion with God which Scripture offers? The answer is because of our chronic unbelief. Faith enables our spiritual sense to function. Where faith is defective the result will be inward insensibility and numbness toward spiritual things. This is the condition of vast numbers of Christians today. No proof is necessary to support that statement. We have but to converse with the first Christian we meet or enter the first church we open to acquire all the proof we need.

A spiritual kingdom lies all about us, enclosing us, embracing us, altogether within reach of our inner selves, waiting for us to recognize it. God Himself is here waiting our response to His presence. This eternal world will come alive to us the moment we begin to reckon upon its reality.

I have just now used two words which demand definition. Or if definition is impossible, I must at least make clear what I mean when I use them. They are *reckon* and *reality*.

What do I mean by *reality*? I mean that which has existence apart from any idea any mind may have of it, and which would exist if there were no mind anywhere to entertain a thought of it. That which is real has being in itself. It does not depend upon the observer for its validity.

I am aware that there are those who love to poke fun at the plain man's idea of reality. They are the idealists who spin endless proofs that nothing is real outside of the mind. They are the relativists who like to show that there are no fixed points in the universe from which we can measure anything. They smile down upon us from their lofty intellectual peaks and settle us to their own satisfaction by fastening upon us the reproachful term "absolutist." The Christian is not put out of countenance by this show of contempt. He can smile right back at them, for he knows that there is only One who is Absolute, that is God. But he knows also that the Absolute One has made this world for man's use, and while there is nothing fixed or real in the last meaning of the words (the meaning as applied to God), *for every purpose of human life we are permitted to act as if there were.* And every man does act thus except the mentally sick. These unfortunates also have trouble with reality, but they are consistent; they insist upon living in accordance with their ideas of things. They are honest, and it is their very honesty which constitutes them a social problem.

The idealists and relativists are not mentally sick. They prove their soundness by living their lives according to the very notions of reality which they in theory repudiate and by counting upon the very fixed points which they prove are not there. They could earn a lot more respect for their notions if they were willing to live by them; but this they are careful not to do. Their ideas are brain-deep, not life-deep. Wherever life touches them they repudiate their theories and live like other men.

The Christian is too sincere to play with ideas for their own sake. He takes no pleasure in the mere spinning of gossamer webs for display. All his beliefs are practical. They are geared into his life. By them he lives or dies, stands or falls for this world and for all time to come. From the insincere man he turns away.

The sincere, plain man knows that the world is real. He finds it here when he wakes to consciousness, and he knows that he did not think it into being. It was here waiting for him when he came, and he knows that when he prepares to leave this earthly scene it will be here still to bid him goodbye as he departs. By the deep wisdom of life he is wiser than a thousand men who doubt. He stands upon the earth and feels the wind and rain in his face, and he knows that they are real. He sees the sun by day and the stars by night. He sees the hot lightning play out of the dark thundercloud. He hears the sounds of nature and the cries of human joy and pain. These he knows are real. He lies down on the cool earth at night and has no fear that it will prove illusory or fail him while he sleeps. In the morning the firm ground will be under him, the blue sky above him and the rocks and trees around him as when he closed his eyes the night before. So he lives and rejoices in a world of reality.

With his five senses he engages this real world. All things necessary to his physical existence he apprehends by the faculties with which he has been equipped by the God who created him and placed him in such a world as this.

Now by our definition also God is real. He is real in the absolute and final sense that nothing else is. All other reality is contingent upon His. The great Reality is God, the Author of that lower and dependent reality which makes up the sum of created things, including ourselves. God has objective existence independent of and apart from any notions which we may have concerning Him. The worshiping heart does not create its Object. It finds Him here when it wakes from its mortal slumber in the morning of its regeneration.

Another word that must be cleared up is *reckon*. This does not mean to visualize or imagine. Imagination is not faith. The two are not only different from, but stand in sharp opposition to, each other. Imagination projects unreal images out of the mind and seeks to attach reality to them. Faith creates nothing; it simply reckons upon that which is already there.

God and the spiritual world are real. We can reckon upon them with as much assurance as we reckon upon the familiar world around us. Spiritual things are there (or rather we should say here) inviting our attention and challenging our trust.

Our trouble is that we have established bad thought habits. We habitually think of the visible world as real and doubt the reality of any other. We do not deny the existence of the spiritual world but we doubt that it is real in the accepted meaning of the word.

The world of sense intrudes upon our attention day and night for the whole of our lifetime. It is clamorous, insistent and self- demonstrating. It does not appeal to our faith; it is here, assaulting our five senses, demanding to be accepted as real and final. But sin has so clouded the lenses of our hearts that we cannot see that other reality, the City of God, shining around us. The world of sense triumphs. The visible becomes the enemy of the invisible, the temporal, of the eternal. That is the curse inherited by every member of Adam's tragic race.

At the root of the Christian life lies belief in the invisible. The object of the Christians's faith is unseen reality.

Our uncorrected thinking, influenced by the blindness of our natural hearts and the intrusive ubiquity of visible things, tends to draw a contrast between the spiritual and the real—but actually no such contrast exists. The antithesis lies elsewhere—between the real and the imaginary, between the spiritual and the material, between the temporal and the eternal; but between the spiritual and the real, never. The spiritual is real.

If we would rise into that region of light and power plainly beckoning us through the Scriptures of truth, we must break the evil habit of ignoring the spiritual. We must shift our interest from the seen to the unseen. For the great unseen Reality is God. "He that cometh to God must believe that he is, and that he is a rewarder of them that diligently seek him" (Hebrews 11:6). This is basic in the life of faith. From there we can rise to unlimited heights. "Ye believe in God," said our Lord Jesus Christ, "believe also in me" (John 14:1). Without the first there can be no second.

If we truly want to follow God, we must seek to be other-worldly. This I say knowing well that word has been used with scorn by the sons of this world and applied to the Christian as a badge of reproach. So be it. Every man must choose his world. If we who follow Christ, with all the facts before us and knowing what we are about, deliberately choose the kingdom of God as our sphere of interest, I see no reason why anyone should object. If we lose by it, the loss is our own; if we gain, we rob no one by so doing. The "other world," which is the object of this world's disdain and the subject of the drunkard's mocking song, is our carefully chosen goal and the object of our holiest longing.

But we must avoid the common fault of pushing the "other world" into the future. It is not future, but present. It parallels our familiar physical world, and the doors between the two worlds are open. "Ye are come," says the writer to the Hebrews (and the tense is plainly present),

> unto mount Sion, and unto the city of the living God, the heavenly Jerusalem, and to an innumerable company of angels, to the general assembly and church of the firstborn, which are written in heaven, and to God the Judge of all, and to the spirits of just men made perfect, and to Jesus the mediator of the new covenant, and to the blood of sprinkling, that speaketh better things than that of Abel. (Hebrews 12:22–24)

All these things are contrasted with "the mount that might be touched" (12:18) and "the sound of a trumpet, and the voice of words" (12:19) that might be heard. May we not safely conclude that, as the realities of Mount Sinai were apprehended by the senses, so the realities of Mount Zion are to be grasped by the soul? And this not by any trick of the imagination but in downright actuality. The soul has eyes with which to see and ears with which to hear. Feeble they may be from long disuse, but by the life-giving touch of Christ they are now alive and capable of sharpest sight and most sensitive hearing.

As we begin to focus upon God, the things of the spirit will take shape before our inner eyes. Obedience to the word of Christ will bring an inward revelation of the Godhead (John 14:21–23). It will give acute perception enabling us to see God even as is promised to the pure in heart. A new God-consciousness will seize upon us and we shall begin to taste and hear and inwardly feel God, who is our life and our all. There will be seen the constant shining of "the true Light, which lighteth every man that cometh into the world" (John 1:9). More and more, as our faculties grow sharper and more sure, God will become to us the great All, and His presence the glory and wonder of our lives.

*   *   *

O God, quicken to life every power within me, that I may lay hold on eternal things. Open my eyes that I may see; give me acute spiritual perception; enable me to taste Thee and know that Thou art good. Make heaven more real to me than earthly thing has ever been.
Amen.

The Universal Presence

Whither shall I go from thy spirit? or whither shall I flee from thy presence? (Psalm 139:7)

In all Christian teaching certain basic truths are found, hidden at times, and rather assumed than asserted, but necessary to all truth as the primary colors are found in and necessary to the finished painting. Such a truth is the divine immanence.

God dwells in His creation and is everywhere indivisibly present in all His works. This is boldly taught by prophet and apostle, and is accepted by Christian theology generally. That is, it appears in the books, but for some reason it has not sunk into the average Christian's heart so as to become a part of his believing self. Christian teachers shy away from its full implications and, if they mention it at all, mute it down till it has little meaning. I would guess the reason for this to be the fear of being charged with pantheism. But the doctrine of the divine Presence is definitely not pantheism.

Pantheism's error is too palpable to deceive anyone. It is that God is the sum of all created things. Nature and God are one, so that whoever touches a leaf or a stone touches God. That is, of course, to degrade the glory of the incorruptible Deity and, in an effort to make all things divine, banish all divinity from the world entirely.

The truth is that while God dwells in His world He is separated from it by a gulf forever impassable. However closely He may be identified with the work of His hands, they are and must eternally be other than He, and He is and must be antecedent to and independent of them. He is transcendent above all His works even while He is immanent within them.

What does the divine immanence mean in direct Christian experience? It means simply that *God is here*. Wherever we are, God is here. There is no place, there can be no place, where He is not. Ten million intelligences standing at as many points in space and separated by incomprehensible distances can each one say with equal truth, God is here. No point is nearer to God than any other point. It is exactly as near to God from any place as it is from any other place. No one is in mere distance any further from or any nearer to God than any other person.

These are truths believed by every instructed Christian. It remains for us to think on them and pray over them until they begin to glow within us.

"In the beginning God . . ." (Genesis 1:1). Not matter, for matter is not self-causing. It requires an antecedent cause, and God is that Cause. Not law, for law is but a name for the course which all creation follows. That course had to be planned, and the Planner is God. Not mind, for mind also is a created thing and must have a Creator back of it. In the beginning God, the uncaused Cause of matter, mind and law. There we must begin.

Adam sinned and, in his panic, frantically tried to do the impossible; he tried to hide from the presence of God. David also must have had wild thoughts of trying to escape from the Presence, for he wrote, "Whither shall I go from thy spirit? or whither shall I flee from thy presence?" (Psalm 139:7). Then he proceeded through one of his most beautiful psalms to celebrate the glory of the divine immanence. "If I ascend up into heaven, thou art there: if I make my bed in hell, behold, thou art there. If I take the wings of the morning, and dwell in the uttermost parts of the sea; even there shall thy hand lead me, and thy right hand shall hold me" (139:8–10). And he knew that God's *being* and God's *seeing* are the same, that the seeing Presence had been with him even before he was born, watching the mystery of unfolding life. Solomon exclaimed, "But will God indeed dwell on the earth? behold, the heaven and heaven of heavens cannot contain thee; how much less this house that I have builded" (1 Kings 8:27). Paul assured the Athenians that "he be not far from every one of us: for in him we live, and move, and have our being" (Acts 17:27–28).

If God is present at every point in space, if we cannot go where He is not, cannot even conceive of a place where He is not, why then has not that Presence become the one universally celebrated fact of the world? The patriarch Jacob, "in the waste howling wilderness" (Deuteronomy 32:10), gave the answer to that question. He saw a vision of God and cried out in wonder, "Surely the LORD is in this place; and I knew it not" (Genesis 28:16). Jacob had never been for one small division of a moment outside the circle of that all-pervading Presence. But he knew it not. That was his trouble, and it is ours. Men do not know that God is here. What a difference it would make if they knew.

The Presence and the manifestation of the Presence are not the same. There can be the one without the other. God is here when we are wholly unaware of it. He is manifest only when and as we are aware of His presence. On our part, there must be surrender to the Spirit of God, for His work is to show us the Father and the Son. If we cooperate with Him in loving obedience, God will manifest Himself to us, and that manifestation will be the difference between a nominal Christian life and a life radiant with the light of His face.

Always, everywhere God is present, and always He seeks to discover Himself to each one. He would reveal not only that He is, but what He is as well. He did not have to be persuaded to reveal Himself to Moses. "And the LORD descended in the cloud, and stood with him there, and proclaimed the name of the LORD" (Exodus 34:5). He not only made a verbal proclamation of His nature but He revealed His very Self to Moses so that the skin of Moses' face shone with the supernatural light. It will be a great moment for some of us when we begin to believe that God's promise of self-revelation is literally true, that He promised much, but no more than He intends to fulfill.

Our pursuit of God is successful just because He is forever seeking to manifest Himself to us. The revelation of God to any man is not God coming from a distance once upon a time to pay a brief and momentous visit to the man's soul. Thus to think of it is to misunderstand it all. The approach of God to the soul or of the soul to God is not to be thought of in spatial terms at all. There is no idea of physical distance involved in the concept. It is not a matter of miles but of experience.

To speak of being near to or far from God is to use language in a sense always understood when applied to our ordinary human relationships. A man may say, "I feel that my son is coming nearer to me as he gets older," and yet that son has lived by his father's side since he was born and has never been away from home more than a day or so in his entire life. What then can the father mean? Obviously he is speaking of experience. He means that the boy is coming to know him more intimately and with deeper understanding, that the barriers of thought and feeling between the two are disappearing, that father and son are becoming more closely united in mind and heart.

So when we sing, "Draw me nearer, nearer, nearer blessed Lord," we are not thinking of the nearness of place, but of the nearness of relationship. It is for increasing degrees of awareness that we pray, for a more perfect consciousness of the divine Presence. We need never shout across the spaces to an absent God. He is nearer than our own soul, closer than our most secret thoughts.

Why do some persons "find" God in a way that others do not? Why does God manifest His presence to some and let multitudes of others struggle along in the half- light of imperfect Christian experience? Of course, the will of God is the same for all. He has no favorites within His household. All He has ever done for any of His children He will do for all of His children. The difference lies not with God but with us.

Pick at random a score of great saints whose lives and testimonies are widely known. Let them be Bible characters or well-known Christians of post-biblical times. You will be struck instantly with the fact that the saints were not alike. Sometimes the unlikenesses were so great as to be positively glaring. How different, for example, was Moses from Isaiah; how different was Elijah from David; how unlike each other were John and Paul, St. Francis and Luther, Finney and Thomas à Kempis. The differences are as wide as human life itself—differences of race, nationality, education, temperament, habit and personal qualities. Yet they all walked, each in his day, upon a high road of spiritual living far above the common way.

Their differences must have been incidental and in the eyes of God of no significance. In some vital quality they must have been alike. What was it?

I venture to suggest that the one vital quality which they had in common was spiritual receptivity. Something in them was open to heaven, something which urged them Godward. Without attempting anything like a profound analysis, I shall say simply that they had spiritual awareness and that they went on to cultivate it until it became the biggest thing in their lives. They differed from the average person in that when they felt the inward longing they *did something about it*. They acquired the lifelong habit of spiritual response. They were not disobedient to the heavenly vision. As David put it neatly, "When thou saidst, Seek ye my face; my heart said unto thee, Thy face, LORD, will I seek" (Psalm 27:8).

As with everything good in human life, back of this receptivity is God. The sovereignty of God is here, and is felt even by those who have not placed particular stress upon it theologically. The pious Michelangelo confessed this in a sonnet:

> My unassisted heart is barren clay,
> That of its native self can nothing
>   feed:
> Of good and pious works Thou are
>   the seed,
> That quickens only where Thou sayest
>   it may:

Unless Thou show to us Thine own
true way
No man can find it: Father! Thou must
lead.

These words will repay study as the deep and serious testimony of a great Christian.

Important as it is that we recognize God working in us, I would yet warn against a too-great preoccupation with the thought. It is a sure road to sterile passivity. God will not hold us responsible to understand the mysteries of election, predestination and the divine sovereignty. The best and safest way to deal with these truths is to raise our eyes to God and in deepest reverence say, "O Lord, Thou knowest." Those things belong to the deep and mysterious profound of God's omniscience. Prying into them may make theologians, but it will never make saints.

Receptivity is not a single thing; rather, it is a compound, a blending of several elements within the soul. It is an affinity for, a bent toward, a sympathetic response to, a desire to have. From this it may be gathered that it can be present in degrees, that we may have little or more, depending upon the individual. It may be increased by exercise or destroyed by neglect. It is not a sovereign and irresistible force which comes upon us as a seizure from above. It is a gift of God, indeed, but one which must be recognized and cultivated as any other gift if we are to realize the purpose for which it was given.

Failure to see this is the cause of a very serious breakdown in modern evangelicalism. The idea of cultivation and exercise, so dear to the saints of old, has now no place in our total religious picture. It is too slow, too common. We now demand *Pentacostal* glamour and fast-flowing dramatic action. A generation of Christians reared among push buttons and automatic machines is impatient of slower and less direct methods of reaching their goals. We have been trying to apply machine-age methods to our relations with God. We read our chapter, have our short devotions and rush away, hoping to make up for our deep inward bankruptcy by attending another gospel meeting or listening to another thrilling story told by a religious adventurer lately returned from afar.

The tragic results of this spirit are all about us: shallow lives, hollow religious philosophies, the preponderance of the element of fun in gospel meetings, the glorification of men, trust in religious externalities, quasi- religious fellowships, salesmanship methods, the mistaking of dynamic personality for the power of the Spirit. These and such as these are the symptoms of an evil disease, a deep and serious malady of the soul.

For this great sickness that is upon us no one person is responsible, and no Christian is wholly free from blame. We have all contributed directly or indirectly, to this sad state of affairs. We have been too blind to see, or too timid to speak out, or too self-satisfied to desire anything better than the poor, average diet with which others appear satisfied. To put it differently, we have accepted one another's notions, copied one another's lives and made one another's experiences the model for our own. And for a generation the trend has been downward. Now we have reached a low place of sand and burnt wire grass and, worst of all, we have made the Word of Truth conform to our experience and accepted this low plane as the very pasture of the blessed.

It will require a determined heart and more than a little courage to wrench ourselves loose from the grip of our times and return to biblical ways. But it can be done. Every now and then in the past Christians have had to do it. History has recorded several large-scale returns led by such men as St. Francis, Martin Luther and George Fox. Unfortunately, there seems to be no Luther or Fox on the horizon at present. Whether or not another such return may be expected before the coming of Christ is a question upon which Christians are not fully agreed, but that is not of too great importance to us now.

What God in His sovereignty may yet do on a world-scale I do not claim to know. But what He will do for the plain man or woman who seeks His face I believe I do know and can tell others. Let any man turn to God in earnest, let him begin to exercise himself unto godliness, let him seek to develop his powers of spiritual receptivity by trust and obedience and humility, and the results will exceed anything he may have hoped in his leaner and weaker days.

Any man who by repentance and a sincere return to God will break himself out of the mold in which he has been held, and will go to the Bible itself for his spiritual standards, will be delighted with what he finds there.

Let us say it again: The universal Presence is a fact. God is here. The whole universe is alive with His life. And He is no strange or foreign God, but the familiar Father of our Lord Jesus Christ whose love has for these thousands of years enfolded the sinful race of men. And always He is trying to get our attention, to reveal Himself to us, to communicate with us. We have within us the ability to know Him if we will but respond to His overtures. (And this we call pursuing God!) We will know Him in increasing degree as our receptivity becomes more perfect by faith and love and practice.

*   *   *

O God and Father, I repent of my sinful preoccupation with visible things. The world has been too much with me. Thou hast been here and I knew it not. I have been blind to Thy presence. Open my eyes that I may behold Thee in and around me. For Christ's sake. Amen.

The Speaking Voice

*In the beginning was the Word, and the Word
was with God, and the Word was God. (John 1:1)*

An intelligent, plain man, untaught in the
truths of Christianity, coming upon this text,
would likely conclude that John meant to teach that
it is the nature of God to speak, to communicate His
thoughts to others. And he would be right. A word
is a medium by which thoughts are expressed, and
the application of the term to the eternal Son leads
us to believe that self-expression is inherent in the
Godhead, that God is forever seeking to speak Himself out to His creation. The whole Bible supports
this idea. God is speaking. Not God spoke, but *God
is speaking.* He is, by His nature, continuously articulate. He fills the world with His speaking voice.

One of the great realities with which we have to
deal is the voice of God in His world. The briefest
and only satisfying cosmogony is this: "He spake,

and it was done" (Psalm 33:9). The *why* of natural law is the loving voice of God immanent in His creation. And this word of God which brought all worlds into being cannot be understood to mean the Bible, for it is not a written or printed word at all, but the expression of the will of God is the breath of God filling the world with living potentiality. The voice of God is the most powerful force in nature, indeed the only force in nature, for all energy is here only because the power-filled Word is being spoken.

The Bible is the written Word of God, and because it is written it is confined and limited by the necessities of ink and paper and leather. The voice of God, however, is alive and free as the sovereign God is free. "The words that I speak unto you, they are spirit, and they are life" (John 6:63). The life is in the speaking words. God's word in the Bible can have power only because it corresponds to God's word in the universe. It is the present Voice which makes the written Word all- powerful. Otherwise it would lie locked in slumber within the covers of a book.

We take a low and primitive view of things when we conceive of God at the creation coming into physical contact with things, shaping and fitting and building like a carpenter. The Bible teaches otherwise: "By the word of the LORD were the heavens made; and all the host of them by the breath of his mouth. . . . For he spake, and it was done; he commanded, and it stood fast" (Psalm 33:6, 9). "Through faith we understand that the worlds were framed by the word of God" (Hebrews 11:3). Again we must remember that God is referring here not to His written Word, but to His speaking Voice. His world-filling Voice is meant, that Voice which antedates the Bible by uncounted centuries, that Voice which has not been silent since the dawn of creation, but is sounding still throughout the full far reaches of the universe.

The Word of God is quick and powerful. In the beginning He spoke to nothing, and it became *something*. Chaos heard it and became order; darkness heard it and became light. "And God said . . . and it was so" (Genesis 1:9). These twin phrases, as cause and effect, occur throughout the Genesis story of creation. The *said* accounts for the *so*. The *so* is the *said* put into the continuous present.

God is here and He is speaking—these truths are back of all other Bible truths; without them there could be no revelation at all. God did not write a book and send it by messenger to be read at a distance by unaided minds. He spoke a Book and lives in His spoken words, constantly speaking His words and causing the power of them to persist across the years. God breathed on clay and it became a man; He breathes on men and they become clay. "Return, ye children of men" (Psalm 90:3) was the word spoken at the Fall by which God decreed the death of every man, and no added word has He needed to speak. The sad procession of mankind across the face of the earth from birth to the grave is proof that His original word was enough.

We have not given sufficient attention to that deep utterance in the book of John, "That was the true Light, which lighteth every man that cometh into the world" (1:9). Shift the punctuation around as we will, the truth is still there: The Word of God affects the hearts of all men as light in the soul. In the hearts of all men the light shines, the Word sounds, and there is no escaping them. Something like this would of necessity be so if God is alive and in His world. And John says that it is so. Even those persons who have never heard of the Bible have still been preached to with sufficient clarity to remove every excuse from their hearts forever. "Which shew the work of the law written in their hearts, their conscience also bearing witness, and their thoughts the mean while accusing or else excusing one another" (Romans 2:15). "For the invisible things of him from the creation of the world are clearly seen, being understood by the things that are made, even his eternal power and Godhead; so that they are without excuse" (1:20).

This universal Voice of God was by the ancient Hebrews often called Wisdom, and was said to be everywhere sounding and searching throughout the earth, seeking some response from the sons of men. The eighth chapter of Proverbs begins, "Doth not wisdom cry? and understanding put forth her voice?" The writer then pictures wisdom as a beautiful woman standing "in the top of high places, by the way in the places of the paths" (8:2). She sounds her voice from every quarter so that no one may miss hearing it. "Unto you, O men, I call; and my voice is to the sons of man" (8:4). Then she pleads for the simple and the foolish to give ear to her words. It is spiritual responses for which this Wisdom of God is pleading, a response which she has always sought and is but rarely able to secure. The tragedy is that our eternal welfare depends upon our hearing and we have trained our ears not to hear.

This universal Voice has ever sounded, and it has often troubled men even when they did not understand the source of their fears. Could it be that this Voice distilling like a living mist upon the hearts of men has been the undiscovered cause of the troubled conscience and the longing for immortality confessed by millions since the dawn of recorded history? We need not fear to face up to this. The speaking Voice is a fact. How men have reacted to it is for any observer to note.

When God spoke out of heaven to our Lord, self-centered men who heard it explained it by natural causes, saying, "It thundered." This habit of explaining the Voice by appeals to natural law is at the very root of modern science. In the living, breathing cosmos there is a mysterious Something, too wonderful, too awful for any mind to understand. The believing man does not claim to understand. He falls to his knees and whispers, "God." The man of earth kneels also, but not to worship. He kneels to examine, to search, to find the cause and the how of things. Just now we happen to be living in a secular age. Our thought habits are those of the scientist, not those of the worshiper. We are more likely to explain than to adore. "It thundered," we exclaim, and go our earthly way. But still the Voice sounds and searches. The order and life of the world depend upon that Voice, but men are mostly too busy or too stubborn to give attention.

Every one of us has had experiences which we have not been able to explain—a sudden sense of loneliness, or a feeling of wonder or awe in the face of the universal vastness. Or we have had a fleeting visitation of light like an illumination from some other sun, giving us in a quick flash an assurance that we are from another world, that our origins are divine. What we saw there, or felt, or heard, may have been contrary to all that we had been taught in the schools and at wide variance with all our former beliefs and opinions. We were forced to suspend our acquired doubts while, for a moment, the clouds were rolled back and we saw and heard for ourselves. Explain such things as we will, I think we have not been fair to the facts until we allow at least the possibility that such experiences may arise from the presence of God in the world and His persistent effort to communicate with mankind. Let us not dismiss such an hypothesis too flippantly.

It is my own belief (and here I shall not feel bad if no one follows me) that every good and beautiful thing which man has produced in the world has been the result of his faulty and sin-blocked response to the creative Voice sounding over the earth. The moral philosophers who dreamed their high dreams of virtue, the religious thinkers who speculated about God and immortality, the poets and artists who created out of common stuff pure and lasting beauty: How can we explain them? It is not enough to say simply, "It was genius."

What then is genius? Could it be that a genius is a man haunted by the speaking Voice, laboring and striving like one possessed to achieve ends which he only vaguely understands? That the great man may have missed God in his labors, that he may even have spoken or written against God does not destroy the idea I am advancing. God's redemptive revelation in Scripture is necessary to saving faith and peace with God. Faith in a risen Savior is necessary if the vague stirrings toward immortality are to bring us to restful and satisfying communion with God. To me this is a plausible explanation of all that is best out of Christ. But you can be a good Christian and not accept my thesis.

The Voice of God is a friendly Voice. No one need fear to listen to it unless he has already made up his mind to resist it. The blood of Jesus has covered not only the human race but all creation as well. "And, having made peace through the blood of his cross, by him to reconcile all things unto himself; by him, I say, whether they be things in earth, or things in heaven" (Colossians 1:20). We may safely preach a friendly heaven. The heavens as well as the earth are filled with the good will of Him that dwelt in the bush. The perfect blood of atonement secures this forever.

Whoever will listen will hear the speaking Heaven. This is definitely not the hour when men take kindly to an exhortation to listen, for listening is not today a part of popular religion. We are at the opposite end of the pole from there. Religion has accepted the monstrous heresy that noise, size, activity and bluster make a man dear to God. But we may take heart. To a people caught in the tempest of the last great conflict God says, "Be still, and know that I am God" (Psalm 46:10), and still He says it, as if He means to tell us that our strength and safety lie not in noise but in silence.

It is important that we get still to wait on God. And it is best that we get alone, preferably with our Bible outspread before us. Then if we will we may draw near to God and begin to hear Him speak to us in our hearts. I think for the average person the progression will be something like this: First a sound as of a Presence walking in the garden. Then a Voice, more intelligible, but still far from clear. Then the happy moment when the Spirit begins to illuminate the Scriptures, and that which had been only a sound, or at best a voice, now becomes an intelligible word, warm and intimate and clear as the word of a dear friend. Then will come life and light, and best of all, ability to see and rest in and embrace Jesus Christ as Savior and Lord and All.

The Bible will never be a living Book to us until we are convinced that God is articulate in His universe. To jump from a dead, impersonal world to a dogmatic Bible is too much for most people. They may admit that they should accept the Bible as the Word of God, and they may try to think of it as such, but they find it impossible to believe that the words there on the page are actually for them.

A man may say, "These words are addressed to me," and yet in his heart not feel and know that they are. He is the victim of a divided psychology. He tries to think of God as mute everywhere else and vocal only in a book.

I believe that much of our religious unbelief is due to a wrong conception of and a wrong feeling for the Scriptures of Truth. A silent God suddenly began to speak in a book and when the book was finished lapsed back into silence again forever. Now we read the book as the record of what God said when He was for a brief time in a speaking mood. With notions like that in our heads how can we believe? The facts are that God is not silent, has never been silent. It is the nature of God to speak. The second Person of the Holy Trinity is called the Word. The Bible is the inevitable outcome of God's continuous speech. It is the infallible declaration of His mind for us put into our familiar human words.

I think a new world will arise out of the religious mists when we approach our Bible with the idea that it is not only a book which was once spoken, but a book which is *now speaking*. The prophets habitually said, "Thus *saith* the LORD." They meant their hearers to understand that God's speaking is in the continuous present. We may use the past tense properly to indicate that at a certain time a certain word of God was spoken, but a word of God once spoken continues to be spoken, as a child once born continues to be alive, or a world once created continues to exist. And those are but imperfect illustrations, for children die and worlds burn out, but the Word of our God endureth forever.

If you would follow on to know the Lord, come at once to the open Bible expecting it to speak to you. Do not come with the notion that it is a thing which you may push around at your convenience. It is more than a thing; it is a voice, a word, the very Word of the living God.

*   *   *

Lord, teach me to listen. The times are noisy and my ears are weary with the thousand raucous sounds which continuously assault them. Give me the spirit of the boy Samuel when he said to Thee, "Speak, for Thy servant heareth." Let me hear Thee speaking in my heart. Let me get used to the sound of Thy voice, that its tones may be familiar when the sounds of earth die away and the only sound will be the music of Thy speaking voice.
Amen.

The Gaze of
the Soul

Looking unto Jesus the author and finisher of our faith. (Hebrews 12:2)

Let us think of our intelligent, plain man mentioned in chapter 6 coming for the first time to the reading of the Scriptures. He approaches the Bible without any previous knowledge of what it contains. He is wholly without prejudice; he has nothing to prove and nothing to defend.

Such a man will not have to read long until his mind begins to observe certain truths standing out from the page. They are the spiritual principles behind the record of God's dealings with men, and woven into the writings of holy men as they "were moved by the Holy Ghost" (2 Peter 1:21). As he reads on he might want to number these truths as they become clear to him and make a brief summary under each number. These summaries will be the tenets of his biblical creed. Further reading will not affect these points except to enlarge and strengthen them. Our man is finding out what the Bible actually teaches.

High up on the list of things which the Bible teaches will be the doctrine of *faith*. The place of weighty importance which the Bible gives to faith will be too plain for him to miss. He will very likely conclude that faith is all-important in the life of the soul. "Without faith it is impossible to please [God]" (Hebrews 11:6). Faith will get me anything, take me anywhere in the kingdom of God, but without faith there can be no approach to God, no forgiveness, no deliverance, no salvation, no communion, no spiritual life at all.

By the time our friend has reached the 11th chapter of Hebrews the eloquent encomium which is there pronounced upon faith will not seem strange to him. He will have read Paul's powerful defense of faith in his Roman and Galatian epistles. Later, if he goes on to study church history, he will understand the amazing power in the teachings of the Reformers as they showed the central place of faith in the Christian religion.

Now if faith is so vitally important, if it is an indispensable must in our pursuit of God, it is perfectly natural that we should be deeply concerned over whether or not we possess this most precious gift. And our minds being what they are, it is inevitable that sooner or later we should get around to inquiring after the nature of faith. What *is* faith? would lie close to the question, Do I *have* faith? and would demand an answer if it were anywhere to be found.

Almost all who preach or write on the subject of faith have much the same things to say concerning it. They tell us that it is believing a promise, that it is taking God at His word, that it is reckoning the Bible to be true and stepping out upon it. The rest of the book or sermon is usually taken up with stories of persons who have had their prayers answered as a result of their faith. These answers are mostly direct gifts of a practical and temporal nature such as health, money, physical protection or success in business. Or if the teacher is of a philosophic turn of mind he may take another course and lose us in a welter of metaphysics or snow us under with psychological jargon as he defines and redefines, paring the slender hair of faith thinner and thinner till it disappears in gossamer shavings at last. When he is finished we get up disappointed and go out "by that same door where in we went." Surely there must be something better than this.

In Scripture there is practically no effort made to define faith. Outside of a brief fourteen-word definition in Hebrews 11:1, I know of no biblical definition. Even there faith is defined functionally, not philosophically; that is, it is a statement of what faith is *in operation, not* what it is *in essence.* It assumes the presence of faith and shows what it results in, rather than what it is. We will be wise to go just that far and attempt to go no further. We are told from whence it comes and by what means: "Faith . . . is the gift of God" (Ephesians 2:8) and

"Faith cometh by hearing, and hearing by the word of God" (Romans 10:17). This much is clear, and, to paraphrase Thomas à Kempis, "I had rather exercise faith than know the definition thereof."

From here on, when the words "faith is" or their equivalent occur in this chapter I ask that they be understood to refer to what faith is in operation as exercised by a believing man. Right here we drop the notion of definition and think about faith as it may be experienced in action. The complexion of our thoughts will be practical, not theoretical.

In a dramatic story in the book of Numbers (21:4–9) faith is seen in action. Israel became discouraged and spoke against God, and the Lord sent fiery serpents among them. "And they bit the people; and much people of Israel died" (21:6). Then Moses sought the Lord for them and He heard and gave them a remedy against the bite of the serpents. He commanded Moses to make a serpent of brass and put it upon a pole in sight of all the people, "and it shall come to pass, that every one that is bitten, when he looketh upon it, shall live" (21:8). Moses obeyed, "and it came to pass, that if a serpent had bitten any man, when he beheld the serpent of brass, he lived" (21:9).

In the New Testament this important bit of history is interpreted for us by no less an authority than our Lord Jesus Christ Himself. He is explaining to His hearers how they may be saved. He tells them that it is by believing. Then to make it clear He refers to this incident in the book of Numbers. "As Moses lifted up the serpent in the wilderness, even so must the Son of man be lifted up: that whosoever believeth in him should not perish, but have eternal life" (John 3:14–15).

Our plain man, in reading this, would make an important discovery. He would notice that *look* and *believe* are synonymous terms. "Looking" on the Old Testament serpent is identical with "believing" on the New Testament Christ. That is, the *looking* and the *believing* are the same thing. And he would understand that, while Israel looked with their external eyes, believing is done with the heart. I think he would conclude that *faith is the gaze of a soul upon a saving God.*

When he had seen this he would remember passages he had read before, and their meaning would come flooding over him. "They looked unto him, and were lightened: and their faces were not ashamed" (Psalm 34:5). "Unto thee lift I up mine eyes, O thou that dwellest in the heavens. Behold, as the eyes of servants look unto the hand of their masters, and as the eyes of a maiden unto the hand of her mistress; so our eyes wait upon the LORD our God, until that he have mercy upon us" (123:1–2). Here the man seeking mercy looks straight at the God of mercy and never takes his eyes away from Him till He grants mercy. And our Lord Himself looked always at God. "Looking up to heaven, he blessed, and brake, and gave the loaves to his disciples" (Matthew 14:19). Indeed, Jesus taught that He wrought His works by always keeping His inward eyes upon His Father. His power lay in His continuous look at God (John 5:19–21).

In full accord with the few texts we have quoted is the whole tenor of the inspired Word. It is summed up for us in the Hebrew epistle when we are instructed to run life's race "looking unto Jesus the author and finisher of our faith" (Hebrews 12:2). From all this we learn that faith is not a once-done act, but a continuous gaze of the heart at the Triune God.

Believing, then, is directing the heart's attention to Jesus. It is lifting the mind to "Behold the Lamb of God" (John 1:29), and never ceasing that beholding for the rest of our lives. At first this may be difficult, but it becomes easier as we look steadily at His wondrous person, quietly and without strain. Distractions may hinder, but once the heart is committed to Him, after each brief excursion away from Him, the attention will return again and rest upon Him like a wandering bird coming back to its window.

I would emphasize this one committal, this one great volitional act which establishes the heart's intention to gaze forever upon Jesus. God takes this intention for our choice and makes what allowances He must for the thousand distractions which beset us in this evil world. He knows that we have set the direction of our hearts toward Jesus, and we can know it too, and comfort ourselves with the knowledge that a habit of soul is forming which will become, after a while, a sort of spiritual reflex requiring no more conscious effort on our part.

Faith is the least self-regarding of the virtues. It is by its very nature scarcely conscious of its own existence. Like the eye which sees everything in front of it and never sees itself, faith is occupied with the Object upon which it rests and pays no attention to itself at all. While we are looking at God we do not see ourselves—blessed riddance. The man who has struggled to purify himself and has had nothing but repeated failures will experience real relief when he stops tinkering with his soul and looks away to the perfect One. While he looks at Christ, the very things he has so long been trying to do will be getting done within him. It will be God working in him to will and to do.

Faith is not in itself a meritorious act; the merit is in the One toward Whom it is directed. Faith is a re-directing of our sight, a getting out of the focus of our own vision and getting God into focus. Sin has twisted our vision inward and made it self-regarding. Unbelief has put self where God should be, and is perilously close to the sin of Lucifer who said, "I will set my throne above the throne of God." Faith looks *out* instead of *in* and the whole life falls into line.

All this may seem too simple. But we have no apology to make. To those who would seek to climb into heaven after help or descend into hell, God says, "The word is nigh thee, even . . . the word of faith" (Romans 10:8). The Word induces us to lift up our eyes unto the Lord and the blessed work of faith begins.

When we lift our inward eyes to gaze upon God we are sure to meet friendly eyes gazing back at us, for it is written that the eyes of the Lord run to and fro throughout all the earth. The sweet language of experience is "Thou God seest me" (Genesis 16:13). When the eyes of the soul looking out meet the eyes of God looking in, heaven has begun right here on this earth.

Nicholas of Cusa wrote four hundred years ago:

> When all my endeavor is turned toward Thee because all Thy endeavor is turned toward me; when I look unto Thee alone with all my attention, nor ever turn aside the eyes of my mind, because Thou dost enfold me with Thy constant regard; when I direct my love toward Thee alone because Thou, who art Love's self hast turned Thee toward me alone. And what, Lord, is my life, save that embrace wherein Thy delightsome sweetness doth so lovingly enfold me?[1]

I should like to say more about this old man of God. He is not much known today anywhere among Christian believers, and among current fundamentalists he is known not at all. I feel that we could gain much from a little acquaintance with men of his spiritual flavor and the school of Christian thought which they represent. Christian literature, to be accepted and approved by evangelical leaders of our times, must follow very closely the same train of thought, a kind of "party line" from which it is scarcely safe to depart. A half-century of this in America has made us smug and content. We imitate each other with slavish devotion. Our most strenuous efforts are put forth to try to say the same thing that everyone around us is saying—and yet to find an excuse for saying it, some little safe variation on the approved theme or, if no more, at least a new illustration.

Nicholas was a true follower of Christ, a lover of the Lord, radiant and shining in his devotion to the person of Jesus. His theology was orthodox but fragrant and sweet as everything about Jesus might properly be expected to be. His conception of eternal life, for instance, is beautiful in itself and, if I mistake not, is nearer in spirit to John 17:3 than that which is current among us today. Life eternal, says Nicholas, is

> nought other than that blessed regard wherewith Thou never ceasest to behold me, yes, even the secret places of my soul. With Thee, to behold is to give life; 'tis unceasingly to impart sweetest love of Thee; 'tis to inflame me to love of Thee by love's imparting, and to feed me by inflaming, and by feeding to kindle my yearning, and by kindling to make me drink of the dew of gladness, and by drinking to infuse in me a fountain of life, and by infusing to make it increase and endure.[2]

Now, if faith is the gaze of the heart at God, and if this gaze is but the raising of the inward eyes to meet the all-seeing eyes of God, then it follows that it is one of the easiest things possible to do. It would be like God to make the most vital thing easy and place it within the range of possibility for the weakest and poorest of us.

Several conclusions may fairly be drawn from all this. The simplicity of it, for instance. Since believing is looking, it can be done without special equipment or religious paraphernalia. God has seen to it that the one life-and-death essential can never be subject to the caprice of accident. Equipment can break down or get lost, water can leak away, records can be destroyed by fire, the minister can be delayed or the church can burn down. All these are external to the soul and are subject to accident or mechanical failure. But looking is of the heart and can be done successfully by any man standing up or kneeling down or lying in his last agony a thousand miles from any church.

Since believing is looking it can be done any time. No season is superior to another season for this sweetest of all acts. God never made salvation depend upon new moons or holy days or sabbaths. A man is not nearer to Christ on Easter Sunday than he is, say, on Saturday, August 3, or Monday, October 4. As long as Christ sits on the mediatorial throne, every day is a good day and all days are days of salvation.

Neither does place matter to this blessed work of believing God. Lift your heart and let it rest upon Jesus and you are instantly in a sanctuary though it be a Pullman berth or a factory or a kitchen. You can see God from anywhere if your mind is set to love and obey Him.

Now, someone may ask, "Is not this of which you speak for special persons such as monks or ministers who have, by the nature of their calling, more time to devote to quiet meditation? I am a busy worker and have little time to spend alone." I am happy to say that the life I describe is for every one of God's children regardless of calling. It is, in fact, happily practiced every day by many hardworking persons and is beyond the reach of none.

Many have found the secret of which I speak and, without giving much thought to what is going on within them, constantly practice this habit of inwardly gazing upon God. They know that something inside their hearts sees God. Even when they are compelled to withdraw their conscious attention in order to engage in earthly affairs, there is within them a secret communion always going on. Let their attention but be released for a moment from necessary business and it flies at once to God again. This has been the testimony of many Christians, so many that even as I state it thus I have a feeling that I am quoting, though from whom or from how many I cannot possibly know.

I do not want to leave the impression that the ordinary means of grace have no value. They most assuredly have. Private prayer should be practiced by every Christian. Long periods of Bible meditation will purify our gaze and direct it; church attendance will enlarge our outlook and increase our love for others. Service and work and activity—all are good and should be engaged in by every Christian. But at the bottom of all these things, giving meaning to them, will be the inward habit of beholding God. A new set of eyes (so to speak) will develop within us enabling us to be looking at God while our outward eyes are seeing the scenes of this passing world.

Someone may fear that we are magnifying private religion out of all proportion, that the "us" of the New Testament is being displaced by a selfish "I." Has it ever occurred to you that one hundred pianos all tuned to the same fork are automatically tuned to each other? They are of one accord by being tuned, not to each other, but to another standard to which one must individually bow. So one hundred worshipers meeting together, each one looking away to Christ, are in heart nearer to each other than they could possibly be were they to become "unity" conscious and turn their eyes away from God to strive for closer fellowship. Social religion is perfected when private religion is purified. The body becomes stronger as its members become healthier. The whole church of God gains when the members that compose it begin to seek a better and a higher life.

All the foregoing presupposes true repentance and a full committal of the life to God. It is hardly necessary to mention this, for only persons who have made such a committal will have read this far.

When the habit of inwardly gazing Godward becomes fixed within us, we shall be ushered onto a new level of spiritual life more in keeping with the promises of God and the mood of the New Testament. The Triune God will be our dwelling place even while our feet walk the low road of simple duty here among men. We will have found life's *summum bonum* indeed.

"There is the source of all delights that can be desired; not only can nought better be thought out by men and angels, but nought better can exist in any mode of being! For it is the absolute maximum of every rational desire, than which a greater cannot be."[3]

*   *   *

*O Lord, I have heard a good word inviting
me to look away to Thee and be satisfied.
My heart longs to respond, but sin has clouded
my vision till I see Thee but dimly. Be pleased to
cleanse me in Thine own precious blood, and make
me inwardly pure, so that I may with unveiled eyes
gaze upon Thee all the days of my earthly pilgrimage.
Then shall I be prepared to behold Thee in full
splendor in the day when Thou shalt appear
to be glorified in Thy saints and admired
in all them that believe.
Amen.*

Footnotes

1. Nicholas of Cusa, *The Vision of God*, E.P. Dutton & Co., Inc., New York, 1928. This and the following used by kind permission of the publishers.
2. *Ibid.*
3. *Ibid.*

Restoring the Creator-Creature Relation

Be thou exalted, O God, above the heavens; let thy glory be above all the earth. (Psalm 57:5)

I t is true that order in nature depends upon right relationships; to achieve harmony each thing must be in its proper position relative to each other thing. In human life it is not otherwise.

I have hinted before in these chapters that the cause of all our human miseries is a radical moral dislocation, an upset in our relation to God and to each other. For whatever else the Fall may have been, it was certainly a sharp change in man's relation to his Creator. He adopted toward God an altered attitude, and by so doing destroyed the proper Creator-creature relation in which, unknown to him, his true happiness lay. Essentially,

salvation is the restoration of a right relation between man and his Creator, a bringing back to
normal of the Creator-creature relation.

A satisfactory spiritual life will begin with a complete change in relation between God and the sinner; not a judicial change merely, but a conscious
and experienced change affecting the sinner's
whole nature. The atonement in Jesus' blood makes
such a change judicially possible and the working
of the Holy Spirit makes it emotionally satisfying.
The story of the prodigal son perfectly illustrates
this latter phase. He had brought a world of trouble
upon himself by forsaking the position which he
had properly held as son of his father. At bottom of
his restoration was nothing more than a reestablish-
ing of the father-son relation which had existed
from his birth and had been altered temporarily by
his act of sinful rebellion. This story overlooks the
legal aspects of redemption, but it makes beautifully
clear the experiential aspects of salvation.

In determining relationships we must begin
somewhere. There must be somewhere a fixed center against which everything else is measured,
where the law of relativity does not enter and we
can say "IS" and make no allowances. Such a center
is God. When God would make His name known to
mankind He could find no better word than "I AM."
When He speaks in the first person He says, "I AM";
when we speak *of* Him we say, "He is"; when we
speak *to* Him we say, "Thou art." Everyone and everything else measures from that fixed point. "I AM

THAT I AM," (Exodus 3:14) says God, "I change not" (Malachi 3:6).

As the sailor locates his position on the sea by "shooting" the sun, so we may get our moral bearings by looking at God. We must begin with God. We are right when, and only when, we stand in a right position relative to God, and we are wrong so far and so long as we stand in any other position.

Much of our difficulty as seeking Christians stems from our unwillingness to take God as He is and adjust our lives accordingly. We insist upon trying to modify Him and to bring Him nearer to our own image. The flesh whimpers against the rigor of God's inexorable sentence and begs like Agag for a little mercy, a little indulgence of its carnal ways. It is no use. We can get a right start only by accepting God as He is and learning to love Him for what He is. As we go on to know Him better we shall find it a source of unspeakable joy that God is just what He is. Some of the most rapturous moments we know will be those we spend in reverent admiration of the Godhead. In those holy moments the very thought of change in Him will be too painful to endure.

So let us begin with God. Back of all, above all, before all is God; first in sequential order, above in rank and station, exalted in dignity and honor. As the self-existent One He gave being to all things, and all things exist out of Him and for Him. "Thou art worthy, O Lord, to receive glory and honour and power: for thou hast created all things, and for thy pleasure they are and were created" (Revelation 4:11).

Every soul belongs to God and exists by His pleasure. God being who and what He is, and we being who and what we are, the only thinkable relation between us is one of full Lordship on His part and complete submission on ours. We owe Him every honor that is in our power to give Him. Our everlasting grief lies in giving Him anything less.

The pursuit of God will embrace the labor of bringing our total personality into conformity to His. And this not judicially, but actually. I do not here refer to the act of justification by faith in Christ. I speak of a voluntary exalting of God to His proper station over us and a willing surrender of our whole being to the place of worshipful submission which the Creator-creature circumstance makes proper.

The moment we make up our minds that we are going on with this determination to exalt God over all, we step out of the world's parade. We shall find ourselves out of adjustment to the ways of the world, and increasingly so as we make progress in the holy way. We shall acquire a new viewpoint; a new and different psychology will be formed within us; a new power will begin to surprise us by its upsurgings and its outgoings.

Our break with the world will be the direct outcome of our changed relation to God. For the world of fallen men does not honor God. Millions call themselves by His name, it is true, and pay some token respect to Him, but a simple test will show how little He is really honored among them. Let the average man be put to the proof on the question of who or what is *above*, and his true position will be exposed. Let him be forced into making a choice between God and money, between God and men, between God and personal ambition, God and self, God and human love, and God will take second place every time. Those other things will be exalted above. However the man may protest, the proof is in the choices he makes day after day throughout his life.

"Be thou exalted" (Psalm 21:13) is the language of victorious spiritual experience. It is a little key to unlock the door to great treasures of grace. It is central in the life of God in the soul. Let the seeking man reach a place where life and lips join to say continually, "Be thou exalted," and a thousand minor problems will be solved at once. His Christian life ceases to be the complicated thing it had been before and becomes the very essence of simplicity. By the exercise of his will he has set his course, and on that course he will stay as if guided by an automatic pilot. If blown off course for a moment by some adverse wind, he will surely return again as by a secret bent of the soul. The hidden motions of the Spirit are working in his favor, and "the stars in their courses" (Judges 5:20) fight for him. He has met his life problem at its center, and everything else must follow along.

Let no one imagine that he will lose anything of human dignity by this voluntary sell-out of his all to his God. He does not by this degrade himself as a man; rather he finds his right place of high honor as one made in the image of his Creator. His deep disgrace lay in his moral derangement, his unnatural usurpation of the place of God. His honor will be proved by restoring again that stolen throne. In exalting God over all he finds his own highest honor upheld.

Anyone who might feel reluctant to surrender his will to the will of another should remember Jesus' words, "Whosoever committeth sin is the servant of sin" (John 8:34). We must of necessity be servant to someone, either to God or to sin. The sinner prides himself on his independence, completely overlooking the fact that he is the weak slave of the sins that rule his members. The man who surrenders to Christ exchanges a cruel slave driver for a kind and gentle Master whose yoke is easy and whose burden is light.

Made as we were in the image of God, we scarcely find it strange to take again our God as our All. God was our original habitat and our hearts cannot but feel at home when they enter again that ancient and beautiful abode.

I hope it is clear that there is a logic behind God's claim to preeminence. That place is His by every right in earth or heaven. While we take to ourselves the place that is His, the whole course of our lives is out of joint. Nothing will or can restore order till our hearts make the great decision: God shall be exalted above.

"Them that honour me I will honour" (1 Samuel 2:30), said God once to a priest of Israel, and that ancient law of the kingdom stands today unchanged by the passing of time or the changes of dispensation. The whole Bible and every page of history proclaim the perpetuation of that law. "If any man serve me, him will my Father honour" (John 12:26), said our Lord Jesus, tying in the old with the new and revealing the essential unity of His ways with men.

Sometimes the best way to see a thing is to look at its opposite. Eli and his sons are placed in the priesthood with the stipulation that they honor God in their lives and ministrations. This they fail to do, and God sends Samuel to announce the consequences. Unknown to Eli this law of reciprocal honor has been all the while secretly working, and now the time has come for judgment to fall. Hophni and Phineas, the degenerate priests, fall in battle; the wife of Hophni dies in childbirth; Israel flees before her enemies; the ark of God is captured by the Philistines, and the old man Eli falls backward and dies of a broken neck. This stark, utter tragedy followed upon Eli's failure to honor God.

Now over against this set almost any Bible character who honestly tried to glorify God in his earthly walk. See how God winked at weakness and overlooked failures as He poured upon His servants grace and blessing untold. Let it be Abraham, Jacob, David, Daniel, Elijah or whom you will; honor followed honor as harvest the seed. The man of God set his heart to exalt God above all; God accepted his intention as fact and acted accordingly. Not perfection, but holy intention made the difference.

In our Lord Jesus Christ this law was seen in simple perfection. In His lowly manhood He humbled Himself and gladly gave all glory to His Father in heaven. He sought not His own honor, but the honor of God who sent Him. "If I honour myself," He said on one occasion, "my honour is nothing: it is my Father that honoureth me" (8:54). So far had the Pharisees departed from this law that they could not understand one who honored God at his own expense. "I honour my Father," said Jesus to them, "and ye do dishonour me" (8:49).

Another saying of Jesus, and a most disturbing one, was put in the form of a question. "How can ye believe, which receive honour one of another, and seek not the honour that cometh from God only?" (5:44). If I understand this correctly, Christ taught here the alarming doctrine that the desire for honor among men made belief impossible. Is this sin at the root of religious unbelief? Could it be that those "intellectual difficulties" which men blame for their inability to believe are but smoke screens to conceal the real cause that lies behind them? Was it this greedy desire for honor from man that made men into Pharisees and Pharisees into Dei- cides? Is this the secret back of religious self-righteousness and empty worship? I believe it may be. The whole course of the life is upset by failure to put God where He belongs. We exalt ourselves instead of God and the curse follows.

In our desire after God let us keep always in mind that God also has desire, and His desire is toward the sons of men, and more particularly toward those sons of men who will make the once-for-all decision to exalt Him over all. Such as these are precious to God above all treasures of earth or sea. In them God finds a theater where He can display His exceeding kindness toward us in Christ Jesus. With them God can walk unhindered; toward them He can act like the God He is.

In speaking thus I have one fear: that I may convince the mind before God can win the heart. For this God-above-all position is one not easy to take. The mind may approve it while not having the consent of the will to put it into effect. While the imagination races ahead to honor God, the will may lag behind and the man must make the decision before the heart can know any real satisfaction. God wants the whole person and He will not rest till He gets us in entirety. No part of the man will do.

Let us pray over this in detail, throwing ourselves at God's feet and meaning everything we say. No one who prays thus in sincerity need wait long for tokens of divine acceptance. God will unveil His glory before His servant's eyes, and He will place all His treasures at the disposal of such a one, for He knows that His honor is safe in such consecrated hands.

*   *   *

O God, be Thou exalted over my possessions. Nothing of earth's treasures shall seem dear unto me if only Thou art glorified in my life. Be Thou exalted over my friendships. I am determined that Thou shalt be

above all, though I must stand deserted and alone in the midst of the earth. Be Thou exalted above my comforts. Though it mean the loss of bodily comforts and the carrying of heavy crosses, I shall keep my vow made this day before Thee. Be Thou exalted over my reputation. Make me ambitious to please Thee even if as a result I must sink into obscurity and my name be forgotten as a dream. Rise, O Lord, into Thy proper place of honor, above my ambitions, above my likes and dislikes, above my family, my health and even my life itself. Let me sink that Thou mayest rise above. Ride forth upon me as Thou didst ride into Jerusalem mounted upon the humble little beast, a colt, the foal of an ass, and let me hear the children cry to Thee, "Hosanna in the highest."
Amen.

Meekness and Rest

Blessed are the meek: for they shall inherit the earth. (Matthew 5:5)

A fairly accurate description of the human race might be furnished to one unacquainted with it by taking the Beatitudes, turning them wrong side out and saying, "Here is your human race." For the exact opposite of the virtues in the Beatitudes are the very qualities which distinguish human life and conduct.

In the world of men we find nothing approaching the virtues of which Jesus spoke in the opening words of the famous Sermon on the Mount. Instead of poverty of spirit we find the rankest kind of pride; instead of mourners we find pleasure seekers; instead of meekness, arrogance; instead of hunger after righteousness we hear men saying, "I am rich and increased with goods and have need of nothing"; instead of mercy we find cruelty; instead of purity of heart, corrupt imaginings; instead of peacemakers we find men quarrelsome and resentful; instead of rejoicing in mistreatment we find them fighting back with every weapon at their command.

Of this kind of moral stuff civilized society is composed. The atmosphere is charged with it; we breathe it with every breath and drink it with our mother's milk. Culture and education refine these things slightly but leave them basically untouched. A whole world of literature has been created to justify this kind of life as the only normal one. And this is the more to be wondered at seeing that these are the evils which make life the bitter struggle it is for all of us. All our heartaches and a great many of our physical ills spring directly out of our sins. Pride, arrogance, resentfulness, evil imaginings, malice, greed are the sources of more human pain than all the diseases that ever afflicted mortal flesh.

Into a world like this the sound of Jesus' words comes wonderful and strange, a visitation from above. It is well that He spoke, for no one else could have done it as well; and it is good that we listen. His words are the essence of truth. He is not offering an opinion; Jesus never uttered opinions. He never guessed; He knew, and He knows. His words are not as Solomon's were, the sum of sound wisdom or the results of keen observation. He spoke out of the fullness of His Godhead, and His words are very Truth itself. He is the only one who could say "blessed" with complete authority, for He is the Blessed One come from the world above to confer blessedness upon mankind. And His words were supported by deeds mightier than any performed on this earth by any other man. It is wisdom for us to listen.

As was often so with Jesus, He used this word *meek* in a brief crisp sentence, and not till sometime later did He go on to explain it. In the same book of Matthew He tells us more about it and applies it to our lives. "Come unto me, all ye that labour and are heavy laden, and I will give you rest. Take my yoke upon you, and learn of me; for I am meek and lowly in heart: and ye shall find rest unto your souls. For my yoke is easy, and my burden is light" (11:28–30). Here we have two things standing in contrast to each other, a burden and a rest. The burden is not a local one, peculiar to those first hearers, but one which is borne by the whole human race. It consists not of political oppression or poverty or hard work. It is far deeper than that. It is felt by the rich as well as the poor, for it is something from which wealth and idleness can never deliver us.

The burden borne by mankind is a heavy and a crushing thing. The word Jesus used means "a load carried or toil borne to the point of exhaustion." Rest is simply release from that burden. It is not something we do; it is what comes to us when we cease to do. His own meekness, that is the rest.

Let us examine our burden. It is altogether an interior one. It attacks the heart and the mind and reaches the body only from within. First, there is the burden of *pride.* The labor of self-love is a heavy one indeed. Think for yourself whether much of your sorrow has not arisen from someone speaking slightingly of you. As long as you set yourself up as a little god to which you must be loyal there will be those who will delight to offer affront to your idol. How then can you hope to have inward peace? The heart's fierce effort to protect itself from every slight, to shield its touchy honor from the bad opinion of friend and enemy, will never let the mind have rest. Continue this fight through the years and the burden will become intolerable. Yet the sons of earth are carrying this burden continually, challenging every word spoken against them, cringing under every criticism, smarting under each fancied slight, tossing sleepless if another is preferred before them.

Such a burden as this is not necessary to bear. Jesus calls us to His rest, and meekness is His method. The meek man cares not at all who is greater than he, for he has long ago decided that the esteem of the world is not worth the effort. He develops toward himself a kindly sense of humor and learns to say, "Oh, so you have been overlooked? They have placed someone else before you? They have whispered that you are pretty small stuff after all? And now you feel hurt because the world is saying about you the very things you have been saying about yourself? Only yesterday you were telling God that you were nothing, a mere worm of the dust. Where is your consistency? Come on, humble yourself and cease to care what men think."

The meek man is not a human mouse afflicted with a sense of his own inferiority. Rather, he may be in his moral life as bold as a lion and as strong as

Samson; but he has stopped being fooled about himself. He has accepted God's estimate of his own life. He knows he is as weak and helpless as God has declared him to be, but paradoxically, he knows at the same time that he is, in the sight of God, more important than angels. In himself, nothing; in God, everything. That is his motto. He knows well that the world will never see him as God sees him and he has stopped caring. He rests perfectly content to allow God to place His own values. He will be patient to wait for the day when everything will get its own price tag and real worth will come into its own. Then the righteous shall shine forth in the kingdom of their Father. He is willing to wait for that day.

In the meantime, he will have attained a place of soul rest. As he walks on in meekness he will be happy to let God defend him. The old struggle to defend himself is over. He has found the peace which meekness brings.

Then also he will get deliverance from the burden of *pretense*. By this I mean not hypocrisy, but the common human desire to put the best foot forward and hide from the world our real inward poverty. For sin has played many evil tricks upon us, and one has been the infusing into us of a false sense of shame. There is hardly a man or woman who dares to be just what he or she is without doctoring up the impression. The fear of being found out gnaws like rodents within their hearts. The man of culture is haunted by the fear that he will someday come upon a man more cultured than himself. The learned man fears to meet a man more learned than he. The rich man sweats under the fear that his clothes or his car or his house will sometime be made to look cheap by comparison with those of another rich man. So-called "society" runs by a motivation not higher than this, and the poorer classes on their level are little better.

Let no one smile this off. These burdens are real, and little by little they kill the victims of this evil and unnatural way of life. And the psychology created by years of this kind of thing makes true meekness seem as unreal as a dream, as aloof as a star. To all the victims of the gnawing disease Jesus says, "Ye . . . [must] become as little children" (Matthew 18:3). For little children do not compare; they receive direct enjoyment from what they have without relating it to something else or someone else. Only as they get older and sin begins to stir within their hearts do jealousy and envy appear. Then they are unable to enjoy what they have if someone else has something larger or better. At that early age does the galling burden come down upon their tender souls, and it never leaves them till Jesus sets them free.

Another source of burden is *artificiality*. I am sure that most people live in secret fear that some day they will be careless and by chance an enemy or friend will be allowed to peep into their poor, empty souls. So they are never relaxed. Bright people are tense and alert in fear that they may be trapped into saying something common or stupid. Traveled people are afraid that they may meet some Marco Polo who is able to describe some remote place where they have never been.

This unnatural condition is part of our sad heritage of sin, but in our day it is aggravated by our whole way of life. Advertising is largely based upon this habit of pretense. "Courses" are offered in this or that field of human learning frankly appealing to the victim's desire to shine at a party. Books are sold, clothes and cosmetics are peddled by playing continually upon this desire to appear what we are not. Artificiality is one curse that will drop away the moment we kneel at Jesus' feet and surrender ourselves to His meekness. Then we will not care what people think of us so long as God is pleased. Then *what we are* will be everything; what we appear will take its place far down the scale of interest for us. Apart from sin we have nothing of which to be ashamed. Only an evil desire to shine makes us want to appear other than we are.

The heart of the world is breaking under this load of pride and pretense. There is no release from our burden apart from the meekness of Christ. Good, keen reasoning may help slightly, but so strong is the vice that if we push it down one place, it will come up somewhere else. To men and women everywhere Jesus says, "Come unto me, and I will give you rest." The rest He offers is the rest of meekness, the blessed relief which comes when we accept ourselves for what we are and cease to pretend. It will take some courage at first, but the needed grace will come as we learn that we are sharing this new and easy yoke with the strong Son of God Himself. He calls it "My yoke," and He walks at one end while we walk at the other.

*   *   *

*Lord, make me childlike. Deliver me from
the urge to compete with another for place or prestige
or position. I would be simple and artless as a little
child. Deliver me from pose and pretense. Forgive me
for thinking of myself. Help me to forget myself and
find my true peace in beholding Thee. That Thou
may answer this prayer I humble myself before Thee.
Lay upon me Thy easy yoke of self-forgetfulness
that through it I may find rest.
Amen.*

The Sacrament of Living

Whether therefore ye eat, or drink, or whatsoever ye do, do all to the glory of God. (1 Corinthians 10:31)

One of the greatest hindrances to internal peace which the Christian encounters is the common habit of dividing our lives into two areas—the sacred and the secular. As these areas are conceived to exist apart from each other and to be morally and spiritually incompatible, and as we are compelled by the necessities of living to be always crossing back and forth from the one to the other, our inner lives tend to break up so that we live a divided instead of a unified life.

Our trouble springs from the fact that we who follow Christ inhabit at once two worlds—the spiritual and the natural. As children of Adam we live our lives on earth subject to the limitations of the flesh and the weaknesses and ills to which human nature is heir. Merely to live among men requires of us years of hard toil and much care and attention to the things of this world. In sharp contrast to this is our life in the Spirit. There we enjoy another and higher kind of life—we are children of God; we possess heavenly status and enjoy intimate fellowship with Christ.

This tends to divide our total life into two departments. We come unconsciously to recognize two sets of actions. The first are performed with a feeling of satisfaction and a firm assurance that they are pleasing to God. These are the sacred acts and they are usually thought to be prayer, Bible reading, hymn singing, church attendance and such other acts as spring directly from faith. They may be known by the fact that they have no direct relation to this world, and would have no meaning whatever except as faith shows us another world, "an house not made with hands, eternal in the heavens" (2 Corinthians 5:1).

Over against these sacred acts are the secular ones. They include all of the ordinary activities of life which we share with the sons and daughters of Adam: eating, sleeping, working, looking after the needs of the body and performing our dull and prosaic duties here on earth. These we often do reluctantly and with many misgivings, often apologizing to God for what we consider a waste of time and strength. The upshot of this is that we are uneasy most of the time. We go about our common tasks with a feeling of deep frustration, telling ourselves pensively that there's a better day coming when we shall slough off this earthly shell and be bothered no more with the affairs of this world.

This is the old sacred-secular antithesis. Most Christians are caught in its trap. They cannot get a satisfactory adjustment between the claims of the two worlds. They try to walk the tightrope between two kingdoms and they find no peace in either. Their strength is reduced, their outlook confused and their joy taken from them.

I believe this state of affairs to be wholly unnecessary. We have gotten ourselves on the horns of a dilemma, true enough, but the dilemma is not real. It is a creature of misunderstanding. The sacred-secular antithesis has no foundation in the New Testament. Without doubt, a more perfect understanding of Christian truth will deliver us from it.

The Lord Jesus Christ Himself is our perfect example, and He knew no divided life. In the presence of His Father He lived on earth without strain from babyhood to His death on the cross. God accepted the offering of His total life, and made no distinction between act and act. "I do always those things that please him," was His brief summary of His own life as it related to the Father (John 8:29). As He moved among men He was poised and restful. What pressure and suffering He endured grew out of His position as the world's sin bearer; they were never the result of moral uncertainty or spiritual maladjustment.

Paul's exhortation to "do all to the glory of God" is more than pious idealism. It is an integral part of the sacred revelation and is to be accepted as the very Word of Truth. It opens before us the possibility of making every act of our lives contribute to the glory of God. Lest we should be too timid to include everything, Paul mentions specifically eating and drinking. This humble privilege we share with the beasts that perish. If these lowly animal acts can be so performed as to honor God, then it becomes difficult to conceive of one that cannot.

That monkish hatred of the body which figures so prominently in the works of certain early devotional writers is wholly without support in the Word of God. Common modesty is found in the sacred Scriptures, it is true, but never prudery or a false sense of shame. The New Testament accepts as a matter of course that in His incarnation our Lord took upon Him a real human body, and no effort is made to steer around the downright implications of such a fact. He lived in that body here among men and never once performed a non-sacred act. His presence in human flesh sweeps away forever the evil notion that there is about the human body something innately offensive to the Deity. God created our bodies, and we do not offend Him by placing the responsibility where it belongs. He is not ashamed of the work of His own hands.

Perversion, misuse and abuse of our human powers should give us cause enough to be ashamed. Bodily acts done in sin and contrary to nature can never honor God. Wherever the human will introduces moral evil we have no longer our innocent and harmless powers as God made them;

we have instead an abused and twisted thing which can never bring glory to its Creator.

Let us, however, assume that perversion and abuse are not present. Let us think of a Christian believer in whose life the twin wonders of repentance and the new birth have been wrought. He is now living according to the will of God as he understands it from the written Word. Of such a one it may be said that every act of his life is or can be as truly sacred as prayer or baptism or the Lord's Supper. To say this is not to bring all acts down to one dead level; it is rather to lift every act up into a living kingdom and turn the whole life into a sacrament.

If a sacrament is an external expression of an inward grace, then we need not hesitate to accept the above thesis. By one act of consecration of our total selves to God we can make every subsequent act express that consecration. We need no more be ashamed of our body—the fleshly servant that carries us through life—than Jesus was of the humble beast upon which He rode into Jerusalem. "The Lord hath need of [him]" (Matthew 21:3) may well apply to our mortal bodies. If Christ dwells in us, we may bear about the Lord of glory as the little beast did of old and give occasion to the multitudes to cry, "Hosanna in the highest."

That we *see* this truth is not enough. If we would escape from the toils of the sacred-secular dilemma, the truth must "run in our blood" and condition the complex of our thoughts. We must practice living to the glory of God, actually and determinedly. By meditation upon this truth, by talking it over with God often in our prayers, by recalling it to our minds frequently as we move about among men, a sense of its wondrous meaning will take hold of us. The old painful duality will go down before a restful unity of life. The knowledge that we are all God's, that He has received all and rejected nothing, will unify our inner lives and make everything sacred to us.

This is not quite all. Long-held habits do not die easily. It will take intelligent thought and a great deal of reverent prayer to escape completely from the sacred-secular psychology. For instance, it may be difficult for the average Christian to get hold of the idea that his daily labors can be performed as acts of worship acceptable to God by Jesus Christ. The old antithesis will crop up in the back of his head sometimes to disturb his peace of mind. Nor will that old serpent, the devil, take all this lying down. He will be there in the cab or at the desk or in the field to remind the Christian that he is giving the better part of his day to the things of this world and allotting to his religious duties only a trifling portion of his time. And unless great care is taken, this will create confusion and bring discouragement and heaviness of heart.

We can meet this successfully only by the exercise of an aggressive faith. We must offer all our acts to God and believe that He accepts them. Then hold firmly to that position and keep insisting that every act of every hour of the day and night be included in the transaction. Keep reminding God in our times of private prayer that we mean every act for

His glory; then supplement those times by a thousand thought-prayers as we go about the job of living. Let us practice the fine art of making every work a priestly ministration. Let us believe that God is in all our simple deeds and learn to find Him there.

A concomitant of the error which we have been discussing is the sacred-secular antithesis as applied to places. It is little short of astonishing that we can read the New Testament and still believe in the inherent sacredness of some places. This error is so widespread that one feels all alone when he tries to combat it. It has acted as a kind of dye to color the thinking of religious persons and has colored the eyes as well so that it is all but impossible to detect its fallacy. In the face of every New Testament teaching to the contrary, it has been said and sung throughout the centuries and accepted as a part of the Christian message, that which it most surely is not. Only the Quakers, so far as my knowledge goes, have had the perception to see the error and the courage to expose it.

Here are the facts as I see them. For four hundred years Israel had dwelt in Egypt, surrounded by the crassest idolatry. By the hand of Moses they were brought out at last and started toward the land of promise. The very idea of holiness had been lost to them. To correct this, God began at the bottom. He localized Himself in the cloud and fire, and later when the tabernacle had been built He dwelt in fiery manifestation in the Holy of Holies. By innumerable distinctions God taught

Israel the difference between holy and unholy. There were holy days, holy vessels, holy garments. There were washings, sacrifices, offerings of many kinds. By these means, Israel learned that *God is holy*. It was this that He was teaching them, not the holiness of things or places. The holiness of Jehovah was the lesson they must learn.

Then came the great day when Christ appeared. Immediately He began to say, "Ye have heard that it was said by them of old time . . . but I say unto you" (Matthew 5:21–22). The Old Testament schooling was over. When Christ died on the cross, the veil of the temple was rent from top to bottom. The Holy of Holies was opened to everyone who would enter in faith. Christ's words were remembered, "The hour cometh, when ye shall neither in this mountain, nor yet at Jerusalem, worship the Father. . . . But the hour cometh, and now is, when the true worshippers shall worship the Father in spirit and in truth: for the Father seeketh such to worship him. God is a Spirit: and they that worship him must worship him in spirit and in truth" (John 4:21, 23–24).

Shortly after, Paul took up the cry of liberty and declared all meats clean, every day holy, all places sacred and every act acceptable to God. The sacredness of times and places, a half-light necessary to the education of the race, passed away before the full sun of spiritual worship.

The essential spirituality of worship remained the possession of the church until it was slowly lost with the passing of the years. Then the natural *legal-*

ity of the fallen hearts of men began to introduce the old distinctions. The church came to observe again days and seasons and times. Certain places were chosen and marked out as holy in a special sense. Differences were observed between one and another day or place or person. The "sacraments" were first two, then three, then four, until with the triumph of Romanism they were fixed at seven.

In all charity, and with no desire to reflect unkindly upon any Christian, however misled, I would point out that the Roman Catholic church represents today the sacred- secular heresy carried to its logical conclusion. Its deadliest effect is the complete cleavage it introduces between religion and life. Its teachers attempt to avoid this snare by many footnotes and multitudinous explanations, but the mind's instinct for logic is too strong. In practical living the cleavage is a fact.

From this bondage reformers and puritans and mystics have labored to free us. Today, the trend in conservative circles is back toward that bondage again. It is said that a horse, after it has been led out of a burning building, will sometimes, by a strange obstinacy, break loose from its rescuer and dash back into the building again to perish in the flame. By some such stubborn tendency toward error, fundamentalism in our day is moving back toward spiritual slavery. The observation of days and times is becoming more and more prominent among us. "Lent" and "holy week" and "good" Friday are words heard more and more frequently upon the lips of gospel Christians. We do not know when we are well off.

In order that I may be understood and not be misunderstood, I would throw into relief the practical implications of the teaching for which I have been arguing, i.e., the sacramental quality of everyday living. Over against its positive meanings, I should like to point out a few things it does not mean.

It does not mean, for instance, that everything we do is of equal importance with everything else we do or may do. One act of a good man's life may differ widely from another in importance. Paul's sewing of tents was not equal to his writing of an Epistle to the Romans, but both were accepted of God and both were true acts of worship. Certainly it is more important to lead a soul to Christ than to plant a garden, but the planting of the garden *can* be as holy an act as the winning of a soul.

Again, it does not mean that every man is as useful as every other man. Gifts differ in the body of Christ. A Billy Bray is not to be compared with a Luther or a Wesley for sheer usefulness to the church and to the world; but the service of the less gifted brother is as pure as that of the more gifted, and God accepts both with equal pleasure.

The "layman" need never think of his humbler task as being inferior to that of his minister. Let every man abide in the calling wherein he is called and his work will be as sacred as the work of the ministry. It is not what a man does that determines whether his work is sacred or secular, it is why he does it. The motive is everything. Let a man sanctify the Lord God in his heart and he can thereafter do no common act. All he does is good and acceptable to God through Jesus Christ. For such a man, living itself will be a priestly ministration. As he performs his never-so-simple task, he will hear the voice of the seraphim saying, "Holy, holy, holy, is the LORD of hosts: the whole earth is full of his glory" (Isaiah 6:3).

*   *   *

Lord, I would trust Thee completely; I would be altogether Thine; I would exalt Thee above all. I desire that I may feel no sense of possessing anything outside of Thee. I want constantly to be aware of Thy overshadowing presence and to hear Thy speaking voice. I long to live in restful sincerity of heart. I want to live so fully in the Spirit that all my thoughts may be as sweet incense ascending to Thee and every act of my life may be an act of worship. Therefore I pray in the words of Thy great servant of old, "I beseech Thee so for to cleanse the intent of mine heart with the unspeakable gift of Thy grace, that I may perfectly love Thee and worthily praise Thee." And all this I confidently believe Thou wilt grant me through the merits of Jesus Christ Thy Son. Amen.

The PURSUIT *of* GOD

STUDY GUIDE

by
JONATHAN L. GRAF

A.W. TOZER

Christian Publications
CAMP HILL, PENNSYLVANIA

Acknowledgments

I wish to thank my Crossfire Care Group—Gene, Doreen, Valerie, Barb and Lisa—for allowing me to "test" this study on them. They provided valuable feedback. I also wish to thank the "Good News" class at Summerdale Alliance Church for putting up with another test run. They helped me to refine this study for use in larger groups. I would like to thank Dave Fessenden—my editor, who also sat in on the "Good News" class study—for providing helpful criticism. Even though I am also his boss, he had the courage to suggest the changes that were needed. Finally, I want to thank Rev. H. Robert Cowles for providing invaluable help as an "independent" set of eyes. The insights and input of all of these individuals have aided this study immensely.

Jonathan L. Graf

Contents

How to Use This Guide

This study guide has been developed to help you get the most out of A. W. Tozer's classic *The Pursuit of God*. It should enable you to understand more clearly what Tozer is saying and to apply the truths he sets forth to your own life.

The study guide is designed for both personal and group use. The personal study section (the material that comes first in each session of this guide) should be read after you read the corresponding chapter in A. W. Tozer's *The Pursuit of God*. Let its comments and questions help you reflect on the major points Tozer is making. It will also provide you with additional Scripture to read and study. The group study section offers a lesson plan and discussion questions for those wishing to use *The Pursuit of God* as the text for an adult Sunday school class or a small group study.

Do not overlook the questions at the back of this study guide that go with each chapter. If you are using this guide by yourself, there should be space enough after each question for you to use that section as a work book. If you are leading a group study, you are hereby granted permission to make copies of the questions for your class members or group. (This permission is necessarily restricted to just the pages of questions in the back of the book.)

Personal Study

Whether you are studying personally or as the leader of a class or small group, you will want to begin by reading the personal study section of Session 1. It provides background information on both A. W. Tozer and how he came to write The Pursuit of God. Be sure to complete the "Introduction Questionnaire" you will find at the end.

129

From that point on, the best method of study will be to read thoughtfully a chapter from *The Pursuit of God*, answer the study guide questions corresponding to that chapter and then follow through with the related study guide lesson. Unless you are a group leader, you need not read the "LESSON PLAN—Group Study" section.

Group Study—Leader's Instructions

As you prepare for each session of your class or group, you will want to read the entire section of this guide that coincides with the chapter of *The Pursuit of God* that your group is studying. In other words, you need to read both the personal study section and the group lesson plans.

The group lesson plans are set up with the same subtitles used for the personal study. This is to help you find information quickly. When the activity recommends that you read a quotation from *The Pursuit of God*, that quotation usually is provided in the personal study section of this guide under the correlating subtitle. (The page numbers that follow the quotations are from the current trade paper and cloth editions of *The Pursuit of God*.) The personal study section will also suggest to you things of significance that you will wish to stress.

As we mentioned above, you are permitted to copy the study guide questions at the end of this book, one copy for each member of your group.

If some or all of your group are especially serious about this study, they may want to have their own copies of this study guide. Naturally, *all* members should have a copy of *The Pursuit of God* and keep up with the reading assignments. These lessons, however, are designed so that members who do not keep up with the reading assignments in *The Pursuit of God* can still get some benefit from the class.

Introduction

Supplementary Materials: *In Pursuit of God: The Life of A.W. Tozer*, James Snyder, Christian Publications, 1991; *How to Be Filled with the Holy Spirit*, A.W. Tozer, Christian Publications, n.d.; "Holy Spirit, Fill Me," Fred Hartley III, Christian Publications, 1992.

A.W. Tozer is one of the most-quoted Christian writers of the 20th century. In his period of highest visibility (1940s–1963) he was also one of the most sought-after speakers in evangelical circles. Because of his intimate relationship with God and his fearlessness at saying what God wanted him to say despite the potential unpopularity of his message, many called him a prophet. Chuck Swindoll has called him "the voice of evangelicalism."

At present, there are over 40 A.W. Tozer books in print. Of these, only nine were produced while Tozer was alive. The remaining books are collections of editorials Tozer wrote while editor of *The Alliance Weekly/Witness* (now *Alliance Life*), or are compiled from his sermons. *The Pursuit of God* remains the all-time best-seller of Tozer's works. While official records have not been accurately kept (and many that were kept were lost in a flood in 1972), by conservative estimations, the English version of *The Pursuit of God* has sold over 1.5 million copies. The classic has also been translated into 19 languages.

In order to gain insight into the spiritual depth and strength of *The Pursuit of God*, it is important to look at who this man Tozer was, and how his classic came to be written.

Tozer, a Pursuer of God

Who was Aiden Wilson Tozer and what set him apart? What should we understand about him to aid us in our study? For a full appreciation of the man, you will want to read James Snyder's biography, *In Pursuit of God*.

Tozer was a man driven by a desire to know more of God. In fact he once said to his long-time friend, Robert W. Battles, "I want to love God more than anyone in my generation." To some of us that may sound selfish and arrogant, but for Tozer it wasn't. It simply came out of an honest desire to enrich his relationship with the Lord.

His humility and deep longing for God can be seen in his "Ordination Prayer." He wrote the prayer originally as a covenant with God at the time of his ordination to the Christian ministry, August 18, 1920. Later he revealed it to the world in one of his first editorials in *The Alliance Weekly*. A portion of it reads:

> Lord Jesus, I come to Thee for spiritual preparation. Lay Thy hand upon me. Anoint me with the oil of the New Testament prophet. Forbid that I should become a religious scribe and thus lose my prophetic calling. Save me from the curse that lies dark across the face of the modern clergy, the curse of compromise, of imitation, of professionalism. Save me from the error of judging a church by its size, its popularity or the amount of its yearly offerings. Help me to remember that I am a prophet—not a promoter, not a religious manager, but a prophet. Let me never become a slave to crowds. Heal my soul of carnal

ambitions and deliver me from the itch for publicity. Save me from bondage to things. Let me not waste my days puttering around the house. Lay Thy terror upon me, O God, and drive me to the place of prayer where I may wrestle with principalities and powers and the rulers of the darkness of this world. Deliver me from overeating and late sleeping. Teach me self-discipline that I may be a good soldier of Jesus Christ.

I accept hard work and small rewards in this life. I ask for no easy place. I shall try to be blind to the little ways that could make my life easier. If others seek the smoother path, I shall try to take the hard way without judging them too harshly. I shall accept opposition and try to take it quietly when it comes. Or if, as sometimes it falleth out to Thy servants, I should have grateful gifts pressed upon me by Thy kindly people, stand by me then and save me from the blight that often follows. Teach me to use whatever I receive in such manner that it will not injure my soul or diminish my spiritual power. (*In Pursuit of God*, pp. 58–59)

This drive to know God—to pursue God—often led Tozer to speak and preach on the subject of worship. When it came to worship, He despised the frivolous, the mundane and the shallow. And who could argue with him? He knew how to worship God. His biographer writes:

Once at a Bible conference [Tozer] testified to a spiritual experience he had as a young preacher. "A preacher friend joined me for a walk in the woods for private Bible reading and prayer. He stopped at a log and, if I know him, probably fell asleep. I went on a little farther, as Jesus did, and knelt down and began to read my Bible. I was reading about the camp of Israel in the wilderness and how God laid it out in a beautiful diamond pattern. All at once I saw God as I never saw Him before. In that wooded sanctuary I fell on my face and worshiped. Since that experience, I have lost all interest in cheap religious thrills. The vacuous religious choruses we sing hold no attraction for me. I came face-to-face with the sovereign God, and since that time only God has mattered in my life." (*In Pursuit of God*, p. 161)

Others as well recognized the ability of Tozer to worship. Raymond McAfee, his longtime associate at Southside Alliance Church in Chicago, relates the following experience they had when praying and worshiping together.

Tozer knelt by his chair, took off his glasses and laid them on the chair. Resting on his bent ankles, he clasped his hands together, raised his face with his eyes closed and began: "Oh God, we are before Thee." With that there came a rush of God's presence that filled the room. We both worshiped in silent ecstasy and wonder and adoration. I've never forgotten that moment, and I don't want to forget it. (*In Pursuit of God*, p. 145)

The Writing of the Classic

Every writer has a different method to make the creative juices flow. Some discipline themselves to write several hours a day; some need to get away and write for a solid week or two; some use a special writing pad, typewriter or computer. Tozer was to become a disciplined writer, particularly when he became editor of *The Alliance Weekly* and had the responsibility of producing an editorial for every issue. But in 1948, the year he gave birth to his classic, he was not yet into those disciplined rigors. True, he had written two biographies, *Wingspread*, about Albert B. Simpson, the founder of The Christian and Missionary Alliance, Tozer's own denomination, and *Let My People Go*, about pioneer missionary R.A. Jaffray (both books are still in print). But Tozer didn't think of himself as a writer—he was a pastor. In fact, Tozer had a very different view as to when a person should write. James Snyder, in his biography, quotes him on the subject: "The only book that should ever be written is one that flows up from the heart, forced out by . . . inward pressure. . . . You should never write a book unless you just have to" (*In Pursuit of God*, pp. 121–122). It was just such pressure that produced the book you are about to study.

Tozer had a speaking engagement in McAllen, Texas, a town near the Mexican boarder. Air travel in the spring of 1948 was not yet commonplace, so he boarded an overnight sleeper for the rail trip to McAllen.

At the time, Tozer was struggling with a "burden" God had given him. He was concerned about the apparent shallowness of many believers—people who claimed to be followers of Christ but who had little knowledge of God and little desire to know Him better. Somehow he wanted to motivate these people.

Upon boarding the train, Tozer asked the porter for a small writing table. And secluded in his sleeper compartment he began to write—oblivious of all else.

About nine in the evening the porter announced the last call for dinner. Tozer asked him for some tea and toast and he kept on writing. As he wrote, the words fairly tumbled into his mind. Feverishly he put them down on paper. By morning he had the entire draft of the book that would affect millions of people to this day (see *In Pursuit of God*, pp. 124–125).

None of Tozer's other books were written in quite this same manner. And although his other books have had a very good ministry, none has come close to the success of *The Pursuit of God*.

Your Relationship with God

That is a thumbnail sketch of A.W. Tozer and the writing of his classic *The Pursuit of God*. Does the "burden" that prompted Tozer to write his book find a response in your heart? What about your relationship with God and His Son Jesus Christ? Would you like it to be closer, more intimate? Why not pause right now and ask God to use His own Word, *The Pursuit of God* and this study you are beginning to effect a powerful, lasting change within you.

The Apostle Paul says: "Examine yourselves, whether ye be in the faith; prove your own selves. Know ye not your own selves, how that Jesus Christ is in you, except ye be reprobates?" (2 Corinthians 13:5). In another place he says, "Wherefore, my beloved, as ye have always obeyed, not as in my presence only, but now much more in my absence, work out your own salvation with fear and trembling. For it is God which worketh in you both to will and to do of his good pleasure." (Philippians 2:12–13).

It is important that we continually take stock of our relationship with the Lord—not because we are worried about losing our salvation, but because a relationship that isn't growing is a stagnant relationship and a hindrance to the work of God.

Before you begin *The Pursuit of God* and follow through this study, take stock by answering the following questions as honestly as you can. You may want to write down your answers—and then review the questions a few weeks after you complete this study to see how your answers may have changed. (Note: this same questionnaire heads the study work sheets at the back of this guide.)

1. How does one become a Christian?

2. When did I become a Christian?

3. Did becoming a Christian bring any noticeable changes to my life? What were they?

4. Have I ever had a subsequent experience that I would consider to be the filling of the Holy Spirit? When did it happen? What changes did this experience bring in my life?

5. Do I find joy in worshiping God, both privately and with fellow believers?

6. How often do I gather with other believers?
   a. less than weekly
   b. weekly
   c. twice a week
   d. more than twice a week

7. How often do I read my Bible?
   a. never
   b. seldom
   c. once or twice a week
   d. three to five times a week
   e. daily or oftener

8. How often do I converse with God in prayer?
   a. seldom
   b. once or twice a week
   c. three to five times a week
   d. daily
   e. frequently throughout the day

9. When I pray is it a meaningful time of communion, or do I quickly run through a list of requests?

10. When a problem occurs in my life, what is my first response to it?
   a. pray or ask "what is God trying to teach me?"
   b. immediately turn the matter over to God
   c. think "what am I going to do?"
   d. react emotionally
   e. do nothing

11. If I answered c, d or e to question 10, how soon do I get around to a or b?
   a. very quickly
   b. somewhat soon
   c. not very soon
   d. never

Improving Your Relationship

As you go through this study, you will be confronted with principles that affect your relationship with God. A most crucial starting point is your prayer life. What did you answer to questions 8 and 9? Unless you're a well-above-average Christian, you may not have scored very high on those two questions. Yes, you pray, but has your prayer life been really meaningful? Have you felt as though you were actually communing with God? Tozer will be introducing the idea of drawing near to God. The concept comes from the letter to the Hebrews:

> Having therefore, brethren, boldness to enter into the holiest by the blood of Jesus, by a new and living way, which he hath consecrated for us, through the veil, that is to say, his flesh; And having an high priest over the house of God; *Let us draw near* with a true heart in full assurance of faith, having our hearts sprinkled from an evil conscience, and our bodies washed with pure water. Let us

hold fast the profession of our faith without wavering; (for
he is faithful that promised;) (10:19–23, italics added)

James speaks in similar terms: "*Draw nigh to God*, and he will
draw nigh to you" (4:8a, italics added). But what does nearness
mean? Is it the amount of time—the *quantity*? Or is it the *quality*
of the interaction?

On a visit to Hong Kong, an American businessman had
occasion to ride the subway. The trains were so crowded, he said,
that certain employees were on the platforms just to push people
into the cars so the doors could close. The American said he was
jammed against people on all sides of him—he was "closer" to
more people than he had ever been before. Yet they were all
strangers; he did not know them. He was not really "near" any
of them.

That may typify your relationship with God. You are close in
proximity to Him but you do not really know Him. You go
through motions, perhaps praying for a list of requests you read
off to God. And probably you take time to quickly scan a few
verses or a chapter from the Scriptures. Quite likely you are in
church regularly. But you do not feel "near" to God in the sense
of intimately knowing Him.

Concerning prayer, someone has suggested that most of us
have our focus all wrong. We glance at God and gaze at our needs.
Rather we should be gazing at God and glancing at our needs. If
we want to develop a meaningful prayer life, we must focus on
God and not on the peripherals.

This week, why not try relating God's Word back to Him when
you pray? Often referred to as "praying the Scriptures," this is a
good discipline that helps us focus on God. It also allows God to
speak to us. You might start with one of the Psalms—Psalm 103
is a good one to begin with. Begin by simply, prayerfully reading
a verse or phrase—changing the "his"-"he" pronouns to "Your"
and "You" and the "your"-"you" pronouns to "my" and "me."

Then if thoughts come to your mind and heart to be added, voice them. For example, you might begin Psalm 103:1 by praying:

> Bless the LORD, O my soul:
>   and all that is within me, bless his holy name.
>
> Father God, teach me to praise You more with my inner being, my mind, my soul. Cause my praise to come from deep within me. Do not let me be superficial with You.

Then move on to verse 2. You may not want to pray this way all the time, but see if it doesn't bring a deeper sense of intimacy into your prayer life. Your focus will turn from a "prayer list"—gazing at needs—to the Supplier—gazing at God.

Why not end this first study by taking such a passage from the Scriptures and praying through it?

LESSON PLAN—Group Study

AIM: To cause my students to examine their own relationships with God and to desire to draw nearer to Him.

Tozer, a Pursuer of God

1. Explain Tozer's passion for wanting to know God. It would be a good idea to read the quotes that are provided earlier.

2. After reading Tozer's statement about wanting to love God more than anyone else loves Him, ask: What do you think about making such a statement? Was it a prideful or humble remark? Would you dare to say that? Why or why not?

3. After reading about Tozer's experiences with the presence of God you may want to ask: Can any of you relate a time when you profoundly felt the presence of God?

The Writing of the Classic

1. Pass out copies of *The Pursuit of God*.

2. Explain the circumstances surrounding the writing of the book. You will want to say everything you can to convince your class members that they should read the book chapter by chapter, in its entirety. As we said, the lesson plans are designed so that a student who has not read the assigned chapter can get *something* out of each session, but those who thoughtfully, prayerfully read all that Tozer has to say will derive maximum benefit.

Your Relationship with God

1. If time permits, spend a few minutes looking at the chapter titles in the table of contents.
2. To stimulate discussion, ask: What chapters especially intrigue you? Why?

3. Pass out copies of the "Introduction Questionnaire." [Copy from back of study guide, or type up your own questionnaire based on the one provided.] Allow 10 minutes for class members to complete it. Depending on the intimacy level of your group, you may want to invite sharing on some of the questions.

4. Discuss Hebrews 10:19–22 and James 4:8. Consider together what it means to be "near to God." Relate the Hong Kong subway illustration.

5. Explain the concept of focus in our prayer life—gazing at God rather than at our needs.

6. You may want to open the class up and ask students what they do in their prayer time to focus on God. Present the idea of "praying the Scriptures." If there is time, have them turn to

Psalm 103 and practice praying in this manner. Depending on the size of your class or group, you may want to have the members divide up into two or more smaller groups. Make sure no one feels pressured to pray aloud. Such a person can simply read the verse when it is his or her turn and at the end say "Amen."

Closing

1. Assign Tozer chapter 1 to be read before the next meeting, and pass out the study guide sheet for chapter 1. To whet the appetites of your members, you may want to read an incisive quote from the chapter.

2. Close in prayer.

Tozer Chapter 1

Following Hard after God

Supplementary Materials: *"Weak Thing" in Moni Land*, William Cutts, Christian Publications, 1990.

Do you have a desire to know God better? The very fact that you are reading *The Pursuit of God* and using this study guide indicates to some extent that you want to experience more in your relationship with God. But our desires are often confused and muddy. *What is God's role in developing my desire? How much work do I have to do to improve our relationship?* Chapter 1 in *The Pursuit of God* deals with these questions.

One question is answered in a theological term we call *prevenient grace*. What does prevenient grace mean? Basically this: before a person can seek God, God must first have sought the person. In other words, God puts within us the impulse to pursue Him. It wouldn't be there without the Holy Spirit of God first working to place that desire or urge within our souls (read John 6:44).

But, while it is the Holy Spirit who puts that urge within us, we still have a responsibility: to pursue God. It is our job to do the pursuing (read First Chronicles 16: 10–11; Psalm 9:10).

The Need to Pursue

Tozer points out that while it is refreshingly true that our justification is by faith, there is often a problem with our "easy conversions" of today. A person can be "saved" by mechanically saying a simple prayer. "Christ may be 'received' without creating any special love for Him in the soul of the receiver. The man is 'saved,' but he is not hungry nor thirsty after God. In fact he is specifically taught to be satisfied and is encouraged to be content with little" (pp. 12–13).

How do we get to know someone? By spending time with him or her. You can't get to know someone personally and intimately through one visit. Likewise you must spend time with God if you are to get to know Him intimately. What, according to Tozer, is the essence of genuine religion? Read John 17:3.

Tozer goes on to say:

> God is a person, and in the deep of His mighty nature He thinks, wills, enjoys, feels, loves, desires, and suffers as any other person may. In making Himself known to us He stays by the familiar pattern of personality. He communicates with us through the avenues of our minds, our wills and our emotions. The continuous and unembarrassed interchange of love and thought between God and the soul of the redeemed man is the throbbing heart of New Testament religion.
>
> This intercourse between God and the soul is known to us in conscious personal awareness. It is personal: it does not come through the body of believers, as such, but is known to the individual, and to the body through the individuals which compose it. It is conscious: it does not stay below the threshold of consciousness and work there unknown to the soul (as, for instance, infant baptism is thought by some to do), but comes within the

field of awareness where the man can know it as he knows any other fact of experience. (pp. 13–14)

Are you personally, consciously aware of God? Would you like to be?

This Intimate Relationship Is Personal

Tozer points out that this conscious awareness, this intimate relationship cannot come through a body of believers. Why can't this relationship come through our involvement with a body of believers? What are the benefits of being a part of a body of believers? (List some of them.)

While there are many benefits to being a part of a body of believers, too many people substitute their association with a group for an actual, intimate relationship with God. Again if you do not have a personal, intimate relationship with God, you can. Tozer points out that everyone should come to a point in his or her faith where he or she is as aware of God as he or she knows any other fact of experience. If this isn't your experience, may God use this study to bring you into such an awareness of Himself.

Salvation Only Begins Our Pursuit

Very many believers stop their pursuit at salvation. "Yes, I believe in God and I have accepted Jesus Christ as my personal Savior, but I'm satisfied with that." If only we can encourage those that there is much more of God to experience. A limitless God means there is no end to our pursuit of Him! What a paradox that is: to know God and yet still to pursue Him!

Two examples of individuals who knew God well were Moses and Paul. Yet, both had a strong desire to know more of God—neither was satisfied with his level of knowledge. Read Exodus 33:13–18. These verses show to what lengths Moses went in order to know God more fully. Read Philippians 3:4–14 and ponder Paul's desire.

The Lack of Spiritual Growth

What is deadly to spiritual growth? Read again what Tozer says:

> I want deliberately to encourage this mighty longing after God. The lack of it has brought us to our present low estate. The stiff and wooden quality about our religious lives is a result of our lack of holy desire. Complacency is a deadly foe of all spiritual growth. Acute desire must be present or there will be no manifestation of Christ to His people. He waits to be wanted. Too bad that with many of us He waits so long, so very long, in vain.
>
> Every age has its own characteristics. Right now we are in an age of religious complexity. The simplicity which is in Christ is rarely found among us. In its stead are programs, methods, organizations and a world of nervous activities which occupy time and attention but can never satisfy the longing of the heart. The shallowness of our inner experience, the hollowness of our worship, and that servile imitation of the world which marks our promotional methods all testify that we, in this day, know God only imperfectly, and the peace of God scarcely at all.
>
> If we would find God amid all the religious externals, we must first determine to find Him, and then proceed in the way of simplicity. Now, as always, God discovers Himself to "babes" and hides Himself in thick darkness from the wise and the prudent. We must simplify our approach to Him. We must strip down to essentials (and they will be found to be blessedly few). We must put away all effort to impress, and come with the guileless candor of childhood. If we do this, without doubt God will quickly respond. (p. 17-18)

For many of us this complacency and lack of acute desire is the root cause of our lack of significant spiritual growth. Some cover up this inner complacency by looking for outward solutions: "My church isn't vibrant enough," "My pastor doesn't preach the Word with power," and so on. Then they look for a more "exciting church" with a more "dynamic" pastor, but that isn't the solution to their lack of spiritual growth.

Tozer pointed out (p. 18) that many search for *God-and.* It is the "ands" that we need to strip away. Tozer felt we need to simplify our approach to God. Read Matthew 18:3–4. Remember that God reveals Himself to "babes" and hides Himself from the wise. We need a simple faith; a simple trust with no strings attached. We need to retain that childlike trust throughout our relationship with the Lord.

One of the most profound examples of simple faith comes from *"Weak Thing" in Moni Land*, the autobiography of William A. Cutts, former missionary to the Moni people of Irian Jaya.

Ototome, a young Moni man from Dugindoga Valley was visiting the Beoga Valley, being entertained in the home of one of the locals. Just as a guest in the States might help the hostess by drying the dishes, Ototome went to the woods to get some firewood. There he was struck on the back by a falling tree. He later told us that his back had been broken. The new Christian Damals who were with him said, "No problem. We'll pray for you and the Chief of Heaven will answer our prayers and heal you." They prayed and Ototome got up and walked back to the hut.

"What sort of thing is this new talk about the Chief of Heaven and His Son?" he wondered. "It has power—not at all like our spirit-appeasement ceremonies where we give all that we have and get nothing in return."

While Ototome was still in the Beoga, messengers came to tell him that his little son had contracted diarrhea and was getting weaker and weaker. Again, the new Damal Christians said, "Don't get upset. The Chief of Heaven has power to heal your boy. We will pray for him right now and he will be well again."

Ototome immediately headed home with the messengers, trekking as fast as possible, hoping to see his son still alive. He was amazed when he saw the boy, not lying listlessly in his mother's lap, but out in the village yard playing with friends. Just as the Beoga Christians had prayed. The news of this double miracle spread through the Dugindoga Valley like wildfire. (pp. 135–136)

That God honors simple, uncomplicated faith, there is no doubt. Lord, help our faith and trust to become less complicated and to focus solely on You.

We need to approach God like the author of the old classic, *The Cloud of Unknowing*. Tozer quotes him as saying, "Lift up thine heart unto God with a meek stirring of Love; and mean Himself, and none of His goods. And thereto, look thee loath to think on aught but God Himself. So that nought work in thy wit, nor in thy will, but only God Himself. This is the work of the soul that most pleaseth God" (p. 18). Too often we approach God hoping for an experience or a sensation instead of simply wanting only God. Try seeking God Himself alone.

LESSON PLAN—Group Study

AIM: To cause my students to examine their own desire to pursue God.

Introduction
1. Open with prayer.

2. Using the questions in italics on the first page of this session, discuss God's role in developing our desire to seek Him. Have students read John 6:44, First Chronicles 16:10–11 and Psalm 9:10, then discuss them.

The Need to Pursue

1. Discuss what Tozer meant by "easy conversions."

2. Discuss these questions: *How do you get to know someone? What, according to Tozer, is the essence of genuine religion?*

3. Read the Tozer quote from pages 13-14 of *The Pursuit of God*. Ask: "Are you personally, consciously aware of God? Would you like to be?" Discuss.

This Intimate Relationship Is Personal

1. Using the questions under the heading "This Intimate Relationship Is Personal," discuss why a personal relationship cannot come through a body of believers. List the benefits of being a part of a body of believers.
2. Discuss the fact that we should come to a place in our spiritual life where we are as aware of God as we are of any other fact of experience. Discuss what keeps us from this intimacy—sin.

Salvation Only Begins Our Pursuit

1. Discuss questions provided under this subhead in the personal study section.
2. Read and discuss Scripture provided.

The Lack of Spiritual Growth

1. Ask: "What is deadly to spiritual growth?" Read the Tozer quote from pages 17-18 of *The Pursuit of God*. Discuss.

2. Discuss the problem of "church hoppers."

3. Discuss the concept of "God-and." Read Scripture provided.

4. Read the passage provided from *"Weak Thing" in Moni Land.* Discuss the passage in relation to the concept of "simple faith."

Closing

1. Read the prayer at the end of Chapter 1 together.

2. Assign reading of Tozer chapter 2 and hand out study guide questions.

3. Close in prayer.

Tozer Chapter 2

The Blessedness of Possessing Nothing

Supplementary Materials: *In Pursuit of God: The Life of A.W. Tozer*, James Snyder, Christian Publications, 1991.

A.W. Tozer had a somewhat unusual interpretation of Matthew 5:3. He did not take "poor in spirit" to mean those who are sad and depressed, but rather those who do not let things—possessions—be too important. In fact, they are people who do not even consider their things to be theirs, but God's.

To these "poor in spirit" people, nothing is theirs—nothing they have comes before God in importance to them. This is a very difficult concept to understand. It is even more difficult to allow God to control you totally.

You can say, "Oh, I have turned everything over to the Lord and He controls my life and my things." But do you really practice that? If we knowingly hold back anything, we are still in control. We can say, "But God controls 95 percent of my life, so He is really the One who is in control." Not true. If we are holding anything back, then we are in control, for when we say, "God, you can have 95 percent of me; I'll just hold on to this 5 percent," we are actually saying that we are still the one who decides what to give and what not to give—we are the controller. Possess nothing! Give it all to the Lord for His control!

Giving God Control

To understand this idea, and to support Tozer's view of Matthew 5:3, read and think about Genesis 22:1–18. How does the story of Abraham and Isaac support Tozer's view?

Tozer himself had a struggle similar to Abraham's. His biographer relates this:

> In 1939, Ada Tozer gave birth to a girl, Rebecca. After six rambunctious boys and a nine-year hiatus, in their middle years the Tozers joyfully welcomed Becky into their home and hearts. Years later, in a sermon, Tozer reflected on that momentous event: "She was a lovely little thing. After raising six boys—it was just like trying to bring up a herd of buffaloes—this refined, feminine little lady came along with all her pretty, frilly things. She and I became sweethearts from the very first day I saw her little red face through the glass in the hospital. I was 42 years old when she was born."
>
> Tozer went on to tell how they dedicated Becky to the Lord. "We dedicated her formally in the church service, but she was still mine. Then the day came when I had to die to my Becky, my little Rebecca. I had to give her up and turn her over to God to take if He wanted her at any time. . . . When I made that awful, terrible dedication I didn't know but God would take her from me. But He didn't. . . . She was safer after I gave her up than she had ever been before. If I had clung to her I would have jeopardized her; but when I opened my hands and said with tears, 'You can have her, God, the dearest thing I have,' she became perfectly safe."
> (*In Pursuit of God*, pp. 187–188)

Why is clinging to things one of the most harmful habits in life? What are some things that are hard for people to give up? What things are hard for you to give up?

The story is told about a pastor—it may have been Peter Marshall—who was discussing giving with one of his parishioners. The man had at one time been of modest means, yet a great giver. Now he was rich and he found it difficult to give. He commented to his pastor that giving the same percentage of money now that he used to give simply amounted to too much money. His pastor said, "I think I understand your problem; let's pray about it." Then he proceeded to pray: "Oh Lord, please make this man poor again so he can enjoy the blessing of giving."

You get the point—the more we have, the harder we hold on to it. Statistics show that those who give the highest percentage of their income to charity make less than $20,000 per year. But let's look at what Scripture says about our possessions and their relation to our walk with God.

Scripture to Study

Read Matthew 19:16–30. What does this passage teach about possessing things? Does it teach we have to sell everything we have? How do we give up the things that possess us? What does this passage teach about the "What's in it for me?" attitude so prevalent today?

Read Mark 8:34–38. What truths can be gleaned from this passage that relate to our theme?

Read Luke 9:57–62. What does this passage teach about serving God only when it is convenient for us? What does it teach about our home and family? How does a "home" possess us and become wrong?

Read Luke 12:15–34. What does this passage say about the following topics: life and possessions; storing up our treasures; anxiety and our provisions?

Read Luke 14:26–35. How should you look at your life? Do things control you—wealth, family, etc.—and keep you from God? Would you still follow God if He allowed something precious to you to be taken away, or would you become angry and bitter?

Conclusion

Reread Tozer's prayer on page 30 of *The Pursuit of God*. Can you honestly pray this prayer? What choice are you going to make? What choice does God want you to make?

LESSON PLAN—Group Study

AIM: To cause students to see the relationship between our possessions and our walk with God. To encourage students to "give up" their possessions to God.

Introduction

1. Discuss Tozer's interpretation of Matthew 5:3.

2. Discuss what it means for God to have full control of our lives. Be sure to emphasize the fact that if we knowingly hold anything back from God, we are still in total control of our lives.

Giving God Control

1. Read Genesis 22:1–18. (Note: if you are certain that everyone in your group is familiar with the story, reading the entire passage is not necessary.)

2. Discuss how the story of Abraham and Isaac supports Tozer's view.

3. Read the quote from the personal section of this study about Tozer's difficulty in "giving up" his daughter. Use the questions following the quote for discussion.

Scripture to Study

Have the group discuss each passage listed under this heading in the personal section. If you have a large group, this is a good opportunity to break up into smaller teams. Have each team study and report on a passage. The questions following each passage can be copied and given to each group.

Closing

1. Have your class turn to Tozer's prayer on page 30 of *The Pursuit of God*. This prayer is one of the most intense in the book. You may not want to have everyone read it together out loud because many will not mean it! Instead you might ask for a time of silent meditation, recommending that those who mean it pray the prayer silently; others may want to simply pray for the courage to make that decision to "give up" their possessions to God.

2. Hand out the study guide questions and assign the reading of chapter 3.

3. Close in prayer.

Removing the Veil

"Thou hast formed us for Thyself, and our hearts are restless till they find *rest* in Thee." —Augustine

Hebrews 10 tells us, "Having therefore, brethren, boldness to enter into the holiest by the blood of Jesus, . . . let us draw near with a true heart in full assurance of faith, having our hearts sprinkled from an evil conscience, and our bodies washed with pure water" (10:19, 22). But while we *should* have confidence and we *should* enter into God's presence, few Christians do. Why is that? Why do so many of us settle for far less spiritually than we could have? Remember what Tozer said:

> The world is perishing for lack of the knowledge of God and the church is famishing for want of His presence. The instant cure of most of our religious ills would be to enter the Presence in spiritual experience, to become suddenly aware that we are in God and that God is in us. This would lift us out of our pitiful narrowness and cause our hearts to be enlarged. (pp. 36-37)

Perhaps the very fact that you are studying The Pursuit of God indicates that you have a longing within you to know more of God—a desire to enter His presence. So what steps should you take?

Glorify God

Begin by glorifying God. That is why man was created—to glorify God. Read Revelation 4:11. How do you glorify God? The following are some ways in which we can glorify God. Look up each verse and meditate on it.

- Psalm 86:11–12—walking in truth
- Romans 15:5–6—unity of the body
- 1 Corinthians 6:20—our bodies
- 2 Corinthians 9:13—obedience to our confession of the gospel (following the Word)
- 1 Peter 2:12—keeping life pure, good deeds before non-Christians
- 1 Peter 4:16—suffering
- 1 Corinthians 10:31—whatever we do
- Psalm 115:1—by praising God for what He does and who He is

Take a moment to praise God for His character and His attributes. Meditate on the meanings and implications of *eternal, immutable, omniscient, love, mercy, righteousness* and *holiness*.

Our Position

Why do so many find the Christian life a struggle? Why do so many find it difficult for praises to roll off the tongue? Maybe we don't feel we have anything to praise God for. Name some things which you can praise God for.

Removing the Veil

Read Hebrews 9:1–14; 10:19–23. Meditate on the implications of these passages. We now can enter the Holy Place—the very presence of God.

Tozer was a solid evangelical believer, yet he is often labeled as a modern mystic. He loved reading the mystics and even compiled a collection—*The Christian Book of Mystical Verse*—of their writings. One of the reasons he loved the mystics was because they seemed to understand this removal of the veil.

> They were prophets, not scribes, for the scribe tells us what he has read, and the prophet tells what he has seen. The distinction is not an imaginary one. Between the scribe who has read and the prophet who has seen there is a difference as wide as the sea. We are overrun today with orthodox scribes, but the prophets, where are they? The hard voice of the scribe sounds over evangelicalism, but the church waits for the tender voice of the saint who has penetrated the veil and has gazed with inward eye upon the wonder that is God. And yet, thus to penetrate, to push in sensitive living experience into the holy Presence, is a privilege open to every child of God. (p. 41)

According to Tozer, many of us are stuck in the outer courts. So why don't we enter His presence? What hinders us? Sin—particularly the sin of self. Purity is very important to our personal communion with the Almighty God.

In the Old Testament, before the High Priest entered the Most Holy Place—and that but once a year—a sacrifice had to be made to purify him. In fact, such was the importance of this that tradition has it that the priest would have a rope tied around him when he went into the Most Holy Place. This was so his body could be pulled out if he was struck dead for approaching God with uncleanness.

And so there is still a "veil" in front of us hiding God's presence from us:

> It is the veil of our fleshly, fallen nature living on, unjudged within us, uncrucified and unrepudiated. It is

the close-woven veil of the self-life which we have never truly acknowledged, of which we have been secretly ashamed, and which for these reasons we have never brought to the judgment of the cross. (p. 42)

We must say—*and mean*—Lord, remove the veil. Take my self-love—my flesh—and remove it. But that is difficult. According to Tozer, this self-love is the thread from which this inner veil is woven. This is the reason it is so hard to tear down: the hyphenated sins of self are not something we *do*, they are something we *are*. "Therein," says Tozer, "lies both their subtlety and their power."

To be specific, the self-sins are self-righteousness, self-pity, self-confidence, self-sufficiency, self-admiration, self-love and a host of others like them. They dwell too deep within us and are too much a part of our natures to come to our attention till the light of God is focused upon them. The grosser manifestations of these sins— egotism, exhibitionism, self-promotion—are strangely tolerated in Christian leaders, even in circles of impeccable orthodoxy. They are so much in evidence as actually, for many people, to become identified with the gospel. I trust it is not a cynical observation to say that they appear these days to be a requisite for popularity in some sections of the church visible. Promoting self under the guise of promoting Christ is currently so common as to excite little notice. (p. 43)

Tozer goes on to say that this veil can only be removed in spiritual experience, never by mere instruction. Unfortunately, our problem often is that we wait for instruction. We want instruction. But if we would only *do*! Take heart, God will do the work if we want it done! Our part is to yield and trust. Do we have the courage to let go of all the hidden "hyphenated selfs"?

Insist that the work be done in very truth and it will be done. The cross is rough and it is deadly, but it is effective. It does not keep its victim hanging there forever. There comes a moment when its work is finished and the suffering victim dies. After that is resurrection glory and power, and the pain is forgotten for joy that the veil is taken away and we have entered in actual spiritual experience the presence of the living God. (p. 45)

LESSON PLAN—Group Study

AIM: That my students will see that they can confidently enter God's presence. They will learn some of the hindrances to entering.

Introduction
1. Open with prayer.
2. Read the quote from pages 36-37 of *The Pursuit of God*. Discuss the issue of entering with confidence into God's presence.

Glorify God
1. Discuss why man was created. Read Revelation 4:11.

2. Have individuals read the verses provided under the personal guide subhead "Glorify God." Have the reader of each verse explain the way in which the verse indicates we can glorify God.

3. Take time to praise God for His character and His attributes.

Our Position
1. Discuss why so many Christians find life a struggle, and why so many find it difficult for praises to roll off the tongue. Take time to think of things we can praise the Lord for.

Removing the Veil

1. Have someone read Hebrews 9:1–14 and 10:19–23. Discuss the implications of these verses.

2. Discuss the lives of some who obviously "enter the veil." Have students name people they know or use Tozer's quote about the "mystics." For extra help, use *The Christian Book of Mystical Verse* compiled by Tozer (Christian Publications).

3. Discuss the hindrances to entering God's presence (sin, lack of desire). Use the quotes provided in the personal guide about the sin of self.

Closing

1. Read the prayer at the end of Chapter 3 together.

2. Hand out study guide questions and assign the reading of Tozer chapter 4.

3. Close in prayer.

Apprehending God

An important step in improving our relationship with God is to analyze just what our level of belief in God is. As a start to that analysis, reread the first two pages of *The Pursuit of God*, Chapter 4.

Level of Belief

Are you clear as to the differences between knowing God as an inference, an ideal or as a reality known in personal experience? Where do you think you are in the area of belief?

One of the major problems in Christianity today is that so many Christians say they believe in the reality of God but in actuality they only believe in God as an inference or ideal. Meditate on what Tozer says:

> Christians, to be sure, go further than this, at least in theory. Their creed requires them to believe in the personality of God, and they have been taught to pray, "Our Father which art in heaven" (Luke 11:2). Now personality and fatherhood carry with them the idea of the possibility of personal acquaintance. This is admitted, I say, in theory, but for millions of Christians, nevertheless, God is no more real than He is to the non-Christian. They go through life trying to love an ideal and be loyal to a mere principle. (p. 48)

God as a Reality

To understand God as a reality, it would be helpful to think about why the unregenerated man can't apprehend God. Read First Corinthians 2:14 and Romans 1:20–21. Meditate on the implications of these verses.

Now think about the ways you know God in reality. Perhaps list the experiences you remember where God showed Himself to you.

How can the Christian know God? He or she should be able to know God in the same way that he or she knows the reality of this world. Read the following verses and reflect on the sense that is mentioned: Psalm 34:8; 45:8; John 10:27; Matthew 5:8.

Next it is important to remember that God brings life to the believer—and an ever-deepening awareness of Himself to those who *want* to grow in faith. That word *want* is important to our spiritual growth and our growing awareness of God. The importance of possessing a free will does not end with salvation. If we do not exercise our free will and decide we want to grow, to know more of God, then we won't grow.

For further study in this area of knowing God as a reality, read and meditate on the following verses: Romans 8:10; 1 Corinthians 2:6–16; Ephesians 2:1–7, 5:14; Hebrews 9:14.

The Key of Faith

Remember that the key to developing our spiritual senses is faith. Read Hebrews 11:6. It is also important to understand Tozer's point about the difference between faith and imagination. Projecting unreal images out of the mind and seeking to attach reality to them is imagination. But that is not faith. Faith does not create anything; it simply believes—Tozer used the word *reckons*—on that which is already there.

Faith believes in the world invisible to us. Why is it so easy to believe in the world we can see and doubt the one we can't see? Read Second Kings 6:8–17.

Are there cases today of God's giving special "sight" to see His armies? The following comes from *On Call*, a missionary auto-biography by Dr. David Thompson. It takes place in Cambodia in the early 1950s during the French-Indochina War.

We had been in Kratie for perhaps a year. French troops were garrisoned in the city because it was a provincial capital. One day the French commander received secret information that a large force of rebels was going to attack the French rubber plantations outside of the town of Snoul, 80 kilometers away. Confident that his information was correct, the commander loaded his troops on trucks and raced to Snoul, hoping to surprise the rebels. The purported attack never materialized. It was a rebel trick.

The actual plan was for a rebel force of about 2,000 to attack Kratie where we lived. As dusk fell, a soldier knocked on our door and asked if we would like to come to the hotel where they were planning to fight to the finish. Father thanked him, but said no. Instead, he said, he and his wife would pray. God had not brought them to Kratie to be destroyed before they had done the work they were sent to do.

I remember having to stay under the bed with my sister while Dad and Mom knelt and prayed. Mom said we were very fussy and made it hard for them to pray. As Dad told it, around 2 a.m. a white flare lit up the square between our house and the hotel. The attack on the hotel started soon after.

Bullets flew everywhere. Suddenly, a red flare shot up and burned briefly in the night sky. The shooting tapered off. In the morning there was no sign of the rebels and nobody understood why the rebels had abandoned the attack. The French commander returned later that day from Snoul and was surprised to find the city intact.

In 1955 the French granted independence to Cambodia, returning power to the king of Cambodia. The king promised amnesty to all the rebels who would turn in their weapons and pledge allegiance to him—some of the rebels were communists. On the announced day, the provincial rebels came by the thousands to the town square and stacked their weapons in a great pile. There were speeches and ceremonies all day. Towards the middle of the day, the retiring French commander asked Dad to translate for him while he spoke to the rebel commander. After the introductions, the commander asked the rebel leader, "Why did you not take the city the night we were diverted to Snoul, leaving Kratie defenseless?"

The rebel commander seemed surprised by the question. He remembered the night very well, he said, and suggested that the French commander was mistaken, for when the rebels attacked Kratie they were confronted by thousands of French soldiers. There were troops everywhere—more than he had seen at any other time during the war! Since the rebel force numbered only 2,000 men, they had decided to flee.

With Dad interpreting, the French commander and the rebel leader argued about the events of that night. Only Dad understood what had happened: the army of the Lord had saved us. God's angels had appeared as French soldiers in such great numbers that the rebels withdrew. (pp. 17–19)

If we truly seek to follow Christ, we need to be "other-worldly." For Tozer, that means for us to reshift our focus.

If we would rise into that region of light and power plainly beckoning us through the Scriptures of truth, we must break the evil habit of ignoring the spiritual. We must shift our interest from the seen to the unseen. For the great unseen Reality is God. "He that cometh to God must believe that he is, and that he is a rewarder of them that diligently seek him" (Hebrews 11:6). This is basic in the life of faith. From there we can rise to unlimited heights. "Ye believe in God," said our Lord Jesus Christ, "believe also in me" (John 14:1). Without the first there can be no second. (p. 54)

We need to rise above circumstances and see the Glory of God. May God help us to do so.

A great help in this area of faith and apprehending God is another Tozer book, *Christ the Eternal Son* (Christian Publications), a collection of sermons on the book of John, compiled after Tozer's death.

LESSON PLAN—Group Study

AIM: That my students will learn the concept of thinking "other-worldly."

Introduction
1. Open in prayer.

Level of Belief
1. Begin by discussing the levels of belief in God as presented on the first two pages of *The Pursuit of God*, Chapter 4.
  A. To most people God is an inference, not a reality. They deduce that He must exist but He is not spiritually known to them.
  B. To others God is only an ideal. He is "goodness," "beauty," "truth" or "the creative impulse behind existence."
  C. God is a reality known in personal experience.

2. Discuss the problem that many Christians say they believe in the reality of God but in actuality they believe in God as an inference or ideal.

3. Read and discuss the Tozer quote from page 48 of *The Pursuit of God*, provided in the personal section.

God as a Reality

1. As an encouragement to the weaker members of the class, use Study Guide Question 1 for Sessions 5 (located at the back of this book). Have members share the ways they know that God is a reality. Spend as much time as possible here since this exercise might be the most beneficial part of the class for those who struggle with their faith.

2. Discuss the unregenerate man—Why can't he apprehend God? Look at First Corinthians 2:14 and Romans 1:20–21. Discuss the deadness of man, how that affects his ability to understand God.

3. Discuss how the Christian can know God. He or she should be able to know God in the same way that he or she knows the reality of this world. Use verses that show the use of the senses: Psalm 34:8; 45:8; John 10:27; Matthew 5:8.

4. God brings life to the believer—then an ever-deepening awareness to those who want to grow in faith. Select some (or all) of the following verses to discuss: Romans 8:10; 1 Corinthians 2:6–16; Ephesians 2:1–7, 5:14; Hebrews 9:14.

The Key of Faith

1. The key to developing our spiritual senses is faith. Read Hebrews 11:6.

2. Discuss Study Guide Questions 5 (the difference between imagination and faith) and 6 (why we think of the visible world as real and often doubt the other).

3. Read and discuss Second Kings 6:8–17. Elisha had spiritual sight that allowed him to see the hosts of God.

4. Do such things still happen today? Yes! Read the experience from *On Call*, by Dr. David Thompson, son of later martyred missionaries, Ed and Ruth Thompson.

5. What do we have to be if we truly seek to follow Christ? Discuss what it means to be "other-wordly." Read the paragraph from *The Pursuit of God*, pages 54-55, which begins, "If we truly want to follow God . . ." Discuss what that means and what the implications are. Perhaps read the preceding paragraph that begins, "If we would rise . . ."

Closing

1. Read the prayer at the end of Chapter 4 together.

2. Hand out the study guide questions and assign chapter 5 to read for next week.

3. Close in prayer.

Session 6

Tozer Chapter 5

The Universal Presence

When contemplating God's presence and what the "Universal Presence" means, we may find it easy to misunderstand the implications. Tozer points this out in his discussion of pantheism vs. God's presence.

The Divine Presence

If you are hazy as to the distinctions between the two views, review the first two pages of Chapter 5. Tozer talks about "the divine immanence" or the fact that God dwells in His creation and is everywhere individually present in all His works. This is *not* pantheism, which is the belief that God is the *sum* of all created things. "The truth is," says Tozer, "that while God dwells in His world He is separated from it by a gulf forever impassable. However closely He may be identified with the work of His hands, they are and must eternally be other than He" (p. 58).

The important aspect we want to meditate on in our study is, *What implications about the presence of God are here for us personally? How can we benefit in our personal relationship with the Lord Jesus Christ through an increased awareness and knowledge of the "Universal Presence"?*

Begin by reading Psalm 139:7–10. As a contemplation exercise rewrite the verses in your own words, substituting places and situations that are meaningful to you.

Remember, God knows everything! He is everywhere! At no time—ever—are we away from the presence of God! That should be an encouragement to us! (There is also an implication to ponder: you can possibly fool fellow Christians about who and what you are, but not God!)

Read and meditate on these other verses: 1 Kings 8:27; Acts 17:27–28.

Sensing God's Presence

Of course this raises the question: Why don't we sense God's presence? Tozer responds to this by saying:

> The Presence and the manifestation of the Presence are not the same. There can be the one without the other. God is here when we are wholly unaware of it. He is manifest only when and as we are aware of His presence. On our part, there must be surrender to the Spirit of God, for His work is to show us the Father and the Son. If we cooperate with Him in loving obedience, God will manifest Himself to us, and that manifestation will be the difference between a nominal Christian life and a life radiant with the light of His face. (p. 60)

The issue of being fully surrendered and obedient to Him cannot be stressed enough. Tozer rightly points out that these areas are the difference between nominal Christian living and a radiant Christian life. Remember from Session 1 when we discussed the difference between nearness of place and nearness of relationship? We must strive to be near in relationship to the Lord if we want to have a deeper experience of His presence.

Tozer points out that we can pray for an increasing degree of awareness. "It will be a great moment for some of us," he states, "when we begin to believe that God's promise of self-revelation is literally true, that He promised much, but no more than He intends to fulfill" (p. 61).

Spiritual Receptivity

Think about this question: Why do some Christians experience God in a way that others do not?

Tozer indicates that it is something called "spiritual receptivity." Within those who truly want more of God and truly sense His presence, a spiritual awareness is cultivated! It is developed until it becomes the biggest thing in their lives. Read Psalm 27:8. Do you, like David, truly seek God's presence with your whole heart? The important issue here is that when you feel an inner longing, you *do something about it!*

Did you understand Tozer's definition of what this receptivity is? He says it is a compound thing, a blending together of several elements within the soul—a knowledge of doctrine and theology intermingled with experience. It is "an affinity for, a bent toward, a sympathetic response to, a desire to have." The fact that you are seriously studying this book indicates that you have such a desire. Cultivate it!

And how is that desire cultivated? Tozer says that it is increased by exercise and destroyed by neglect! He also points out that our ignorance of this fact "is the cause of a very serious breakdown in modern evangelicalism."

> The idea of cultivation and exercise, so dear to the saints of old, has now no place in our total religious picture. It is too slow, too common. We now demand glamour and fast flowing dramatic action. A generation of Christians reared among push buttons and automatic machines is impatient of slower and less direct methods of reaching their goals. We have been trying to apply machine-age methods to our relations with God. We read our chapter, have our short

devotions and rush away, hoping to make up for our deep inward bankruptcy by attending another gospel meeting or listening to another thrilling story told by a religious adventurer lately returned from afar. (pp. 64-65)

And how can we break out of a life of dull spiritual senses? Turn to God in earnest! We have within us the ability to know Him if we would only respond to His overtures!

What a difference a simple heart attitude can make. When you approach a Sunday morning thinking, *Oh well, it's another Sunday and I've got to go to church. I wonder how long the service will go today.* That is not the way to meet God—unless He drives you to an altar of repentance because of your lousy attitude! But when you go to church with the heartfelt anticipation of being in God's presence and with the excitement of another opportunity to worship God with fellow believers, you can expect Him to meet you with an outpouring of His presence. Approach God with desire!

LESSON PLAN—Group Study

AIM: To help my students realize a deeper understanding of God's presence and to cultivate the desire within them to develop their spiritual awareness.

Introduction
1. Open in prayer.

The Divine Presence
1. Discuss the differences between a biblical understanding of God's universal presence and pantheism.
2. Read Psalm 139:7–10. Ask some students to share their rewritten Psalm according to the instructions in Study Guide Question 2.
3. Discuss the implications God's universal presence has to our own lives.

Sensing God's Presence

1. Read and discuss the Tozer quote from page 60 of *The Pursuit of God*.

2. Discuss why so many Christians seldom sense His presence.

Spiritual Receptivity

1. Discuss what Tozer meant by "spiritual receptivity."
2. Discuss how it is developed and how it is hindered.

3. Read the Tozer quote from pages 64-65 of *The Pursuit of God*.

4. Discuss ways to break out of spiritual dullness.

Closing

1. Read the prayer at the end of Chapter 5 together.

2. Assign chapter 6 to read and hand out study guide questions for next week's class.

3. Close in prayer.

The Speaking Voice

Supplementary Materials: *70 Years of Miracles*, Richard H. Harvey, Horizon Books, 1977, 1992. *You Can Make a Difference*, Tony Campolo, Word Books, 1984.

Does God still speak today? Tozer would shout a resounding "Yes!" Are you aware of God's speaking voice in your own life? Try to recall a time when you were certain the Lord was speaking to you. If you need more encouragement, read *70 Years of Miracles*, which is loaded with true stories of miraculous answers to prayer and instances of God's clearly speaking to people. Tony Campolo's book *You Can Make a Difference* also has a wonderful story of God's clearly speaking to His people (pp. 24–25).

When pondering this issue of God's speaking, it is important to understand how to hear His voice. In what forms does it come? Can we develop an ear for it?

God's Voice in His Word

One way to hear God's voice is to read His Word—the Bible. Read Psalm 33:6, 9; Hebrews 11:3; Genesis 1:9. What do these verses indicate about the power of God's Word?

What is the relation of God's spoken Word to His written Word—the Bible? To understand this issue, study what Scripture says about God's Word.

A. Jeremiah 5:14, 23:29; Ephesians 6:17; Hebrews 4:12
B. 1 Peter 1:23–2:3
C. Psalm 119:89; Matthew 24:35
D. Deuteronomy 8:3; Job 23:12; Psalm 119:103
E. Psalm 119:11; Deuteronomy 11:18; Romans 10:8; Colossians 3:16
F. Jeremiah 15:16; Psalm 119:140
G. Psalm 19:8, 119:105, 130; Proverbs 6:23; 2 Peter 1:19

God's Voice to the Unsaved and the Saved

The Scriptures indicate that God's voice is apparent to the unsaved. Read John 1:9–10; Romans 1:20; 2:15. What do these verses have to say about God's voice and the unsaved?

God's voice is also apparent to His children in the same ways plus many more ways as well. But we have to tune our ear to it. And that is difficult. As Tozer said:

> Whoever will listen will hear the speaking Heaven. This is definitely not the hour when men take kindly to an exhortation to listen, for listening is not today a part of popular religion. We are at the opposite end of the pole from there. Religion has accepted the monstrous heresy that noise, size, activity and bluster make a man dear to God. But we may take heart. To a people caught in the tempest of the last great conflict God says, "Be still, and know that I am God" (Psalm 46:10), and still He says it, as if He means to tell us that our strength and safety lie not in noise but in silence. (pp. 75-76)

Do you allow enough times of stillness in your life to hear the voice of God? Sometimes we are afraid to be still because we're not sure about God's voice. How did you know it was God's voice that you heard? One sure test is that God will never tell us something that is contrary to His Word, the Bible! If you are not sure it was God's voice you heard, check out what you heard against Scripture. Meditate on His Word—He will give you the certainty you need.

Developing Your Sense of Hearing

Do you want to hear more of God's voice? There are ways you can develop your sense of hearing so you can more closely and regularly hear God's voice:

1. The first and most obvious way is to be still and listen. Establish more silent time as a part of your devotional life.
2. Second, obey God's Word. Allow the Bible to be "a living Book" to you. Deal with the sin in your life. Keep your life pure before God. Develop your spiritual ears through spiritual exercise. Increase your times of Bible reading and prayer.
3. Finally, pray for illumination. At the beginning of each quiet time, ask the Holy Spirit to speak to you. Remember what Tozer said:

> It is important that we get still to wait on God. And it is best that we get alone, preferably with our Bible outspread before us. Then if we will we may draw near to God and begin to hear Him speak to us in our hearts. I think for the average person the progression will be something like this: First a sound as of a Presence walking in the garden. Then a voice, more intelligible, but still far from clear. Then the happy moment when the Spirit begins to illuminate the Scriptures, and that which had been only a sound, or at best a voice, now becomes an intelligible word, warm and intimate and clear as the word of a dear friend. Then will come life and light, and

best of all, ability to see and rest in and embrace Jesus Christ as Saviour and Lord and All. (p. 76)

As a closing exercise, read Psalm 29 and meditate on God's voice.

LESSON PLAN—Group Study

AIM: That my students will learn the characteristics of God's spoken and written Word and understand how to develop their "ears" to hear God's spoken voice.

Introduction

1. Open with prayer.

2. Find an illustration to use as an example of God's clearly speaking to an individual. Two suggestions are given at the beginning of the personal study.

God's Voice in His Word

1. Have students read Psalm 33:6, 9; Hebrews 11:3; and Genesis 1:9. Discuss what they say about God's Word.

2. Discuss the relationship between God's spoken Word and His written Word, the Bible.

3. Assign the following verses to students. Have them explain what each says about God's Word.

A. (Powerful): Jeremiah 5:14, 23:29; Ephesians 6:17; Hebrews 4:12
B. (Purifies): 1 Peter 1:23–2:3
C. (Eternal): Psalm 119:89; Matthew 24:35

D. (Food): Deuteronomy 8:3; Job 23:12; Psalm 119:103
E. (Should be written on our hearts): Psalm 119:11; Deuteronomy 11:18; Romans 10:8; Colossians 3:16
F. (We should love it): Jeremiah 15:16; Psalm 119:140
G. (Brings light): Psalm 19:8, 119:105, 130; Proverbs 6:23; 2 Peter 1:19

God's Voice to the Unsaved and the Saved

1. Discuss how God's voice is apparent to the unsaved. Read John 1:9–10, Romans 1:20 and 2:15.

2. Discuss the ways in which God's voice is apparent to His children.

3. Read the quote from pages 75-76 of *The Pursuit of God*. Discuss the importance of stillness in hearing God's voice.

4. Have students share times when they heard God's voice. Discuss how they knew it was God's voice. Bring out the point that God will never tell us to do something that is contrary to His written Word!

Developing Your Sense of Hearing

1. Discuss the ways we can develop our ability to hear God's voice.

A. Be still and listen. Establish more silent time as a part of your devotional life.
B. Obey God's Word. Allow the Bible to be "a living Book" to you. Deal with the sin in your life. Keep your life pure before God.
C. Develop your spiritual ears through spiritual exercise. Increase your times of Bible reading and prayer.
D. Pray for illumination.

2. If time permits, read Psalm 29 and discuss what it tells us about God's voice.

Closing

1. Read the prayer at the end of Chapter 6 together.

2. Assign Tozer chapter 7 to read and hand out the study guide questions for next week.

3. Close in prayer.

Session 8

The Gaze of the Soul

> But without faith it is impossible to please him: for he that cometh to God must believe that he is, and that he is a rewarder of them that diligently seek him. (Hebrews 11:6)

What is faith? Hebrews 11:1 tells us that "faith is the substance of things hoped for the evidence of things not seen." And what do we have if we have faith? According to Tozer our faith allows us to approach God; through it we have forgiveness, deliverance, salvation, communion and our spiritual life.

Faith Defined

There is an important dimension to faith that we must not miss. Tozer tells us that faith is defined functionally, not philosophically. What did he mean by that? There is a clue in Hebrews 11:1, for this verse shows faith in operation, not in essence. What might that imply about faith? Just that faith is proven in action.

Study the following verses in Hebrews 11: 4, 5, 7, 8, 11, 17, 20, 21, 22, 23, 29 and 31. Notice that we are told each individual did something "by faith." When there is faith, there is an action.

Study these other Scriptures that talk about faith, and notice in each passage what action results from faith: James 2:14–26; Ezekiel 33:32; Matthew 7:21; 1 John 3:11–18. We can safely conclude that if there isn't a demonstration of faith in our lives, we cannot say we have faith.

Obtaining Faith

How do we obtain faith? Read Ephesians 2:8 and Romans 10:17. What do they reveal about how faith is obtained?

To understand faith in action, read Numbers 21:4–9. Compare this with John 3:14–15. What does this teach us about faith today? Tozer points out that "looking" in the Old Testament and "believing" in the New are the same thing! Israel looked with external eyes. Believing is done with the heart and mind. Faith is the gaze of the soul upon a saving God. Compare Psalm 34:5 and Psalm 123:1–2 with Matthew 14:19 and John 5:19–21. What do these verses say to us about faith?

Hebrews 12:2 tells us that we are to look—"fix our eyes," as one translation puts it—to gaze with our soul, to believe, to have faith. For our faith to increase, our gaze needs to increase. Tozer tells us that faith is not a once-done act—it is a continuous gaze of the heart at God.

> Believing, then, is directing the heart's attention to Jesus. It is lifting the mind to "behold the Lamb of God" (John 1:29) and never ceasing that beholding for the rest of our lives. At first this may be difficult, but it becomes easier as we look steadily at His wondrous person, quietly and without strain. Distractions may hinder, but once the heart is committed to Him, after each brief excursion away from Him, the attention will return again and again and rest upon Him like a wandering bird coming back to its window.
>
> I would emphasize this one committal, this one great volitional act which establishes the heart's intention to gaze forever upon Jesus. God takes this intention for our choice and makes what allowances He must for the thousand distractions which beset us in this evil world. He

knows that we have set the direction of our hearts toward Jesus, and we can know it too, and comfort ourselves with the knowledge that a habit of soul is forming which will become, after a while, a sort of spiritual reflex requiring no more conscious effort on our part. (p. 84)

My grandfather is a very good illustration of what Tozer is saying here. My grandfather loved the Lord. He was a long-time pastor, from the old school. Having become a believer when he was an adult, Grandpa never went to Bible college or seminary, yet he knew God and how to communicate to people. I remember fondly the times I spent with him when I was a young boy. Grandpa had an interesting quirk. Often we would be doing something together—playing caroms was a favorite pastime—and Grandpa would get this faraway look in his eye. He would then lean back in his chair, sigh contentedly and say, "Well, bless the Lord!" As a boy I didn't understand fully what he was doing. But now I see. Grandpa had such a rich love for the Lord Jesus Christ and such a deep faith in Him that whenever his mind wandered from what he was doing, it wandered to the things of the Lord! That was the spiritual reflex of faith that Tozer talked about—a faith so rich and strong that our minds simply wander to thoughts of God whenever they wander.

Tozer goes on to add that "like the eye which sees everything in front of it and never sees itself, faith is occupied with the Object upon which it rests and pays no attention to itself at all. . . . Faith is a redirecting of our sight, a getting out of focus of our own vision and getting God into focus" (p. 85).

Remember, too, that faith doesn't need props. It can be exercised in any season, at any time and in any place.

Strengthening Our Gaze

What purifies and strengthens our gaze? Bible reading, prayer and corporate worship. We all accept spending more time in Bible reading and prayer as a means of deepening our faith, but what about corporate worship? While our relationship with God is personal, Tozer indicates that the development of individual faith does something to the unity of the body of Christ—it strengthens it! What a wonderful illustration is provided on page 90:

> Has it ever occurred to you that one hundred pianos all tuned to the same fork are automatically tuned to each other? They are of one accord by being tuned, not to each other, but to another standard to which each one must individually bow. So one hundred worshippers meeting together, each one looking away to Christ, are in heart nearer to each other than they could possibly be were they to become "unity" conscious and turn their eyes away from God to strive for closer fellowship. Social religion is perfected when private religion is purified.

We need more believers who "gaze their souls" on God and not on externals.

LESSON PLAN—Group Study

AIM: That my students will learn that the proof of faith is action.

Introduction

1. Open with prayer.

2. Read Hebrews 11:6 and 11:1. Discuss what faith is.

Faith Defined

1. Discuss what Tozer means by faith being defined functionally and not philosophically.

2. Have students read the verses provided in Hebrews 11 and point out in each what the action was.

3. Study the other provided Scriptures and discuss what each says about the action of faith. James 2:14–26 (Faith without works is dead. If there isn't a demonstration of our faith, how can we say that we have faith?); Ezekiel 33:32 (Action demonstrates our true heart!); Matthew 7:21 (Only those who do the will of My Father); 1 John 3:11–18 (Love is the mark; action is the proof).

Obtaining Faith

1. Have students read Ephesians 2:8 and Romans 10:17. Discuss how we obtain faith.

2. To discuss faith in action, compare Numbers 21:4–9 with John 3:14–15. What do they teach us about faith today?

3. Discuss the comparison of "looking" in the Old Testament with "believing" in the New. Read and discuss Psalm 34:5; Psalm 123:1–2; Matthew 14:19; John 5:19–21; Hebrews 12:2.

4. Read the quote from page 84 of *The Pursuit of God*.

Strengthening Our Gaze

1. Discuss the things that strengthen our "gaze."

2. Discuss the importance of faith to the unity of corporate worship. Use the quote from page 90 of *The Pursuit of God*.

Closing

1. Read the prayer at the end of Chapter 7 together.

2. Assign Tozer chapter 8 and hand out the study guide questions for next week.

3. Close in prayer.

Restoring the Creator-Creature Relation

In order to think about the Creator-creature relationship and restoring it to its intended position, we must understand the effects of that relationship that the Fall left.

Fallen and Restored Humanity

Tozer indicates that the Fall left a radical moral dislocation, an upset in our relation to God and each other. So dislocated did our relationship with God become that we no longer even realized that it is only a proper relationship with the Creator that can bring true happiness.

What are we like apart from our relationship with God? Study Romans 1:20–32. Pay particular attention to verse 25.

After pondering fallen humanity, think about restored humanity. And what restores the Creator-creature relationship? "Essentially," says Tozer, "salvation is the restoration of a right relation between man and his Creator, a bringing back to normal of the Creator-creature relation" (*The Pursuit of God*, pp. 93-94). Read Second Corinthians 5:17.

A Fixed Center

Tozer talked about the importance of "a fixed center against which everything else is measured." Why should God be our fixed center?

In determining relationships we must begin somewhere. There must be somewhere a fixed center against which everything else is measured, where the law of relativity does not enter and we can say "IS" and make no allowances. Such a center is God. When God would make His name known to mankind He could find no better word than "I AM." When He speaks in the first person He says, "I AM"; when we speak *of* Him we say, "He is"; when we speak *to* Him we say, "Thou art." Everyone and everything else measures from that fixed point. "I am that I am," says God, "I change not."

As the sailor locates his position on the sea by "shooting" the sun, so we may get our moral bearings by looking at God. We must begin with God. We are right when, and only when, we stand in a right position relative to God, and we are wrong so far and so long as we stand in any other position.

Much of our difficulty as seeking Christians stems from our unwillingness to take God as He is and adjust our lives accordingly. We insist upon trying to modify Him and to bring Him nearer to our own image. (pp. 94-95)

What does he mean that "we modify" God? In what ways do we? Tozer says the only thinkable relation between us and God is one of full Lordship on His part and complete submission on our part! Why is that important?

Read and meditate on Job 38:1–38, 40:1–2; compare with Job's response in 40:3–5, 42:1–6. For further study read and meditate on the following: Daniel 4:28–37; James 4:6; Proverbs 16:5, 18:12.

What does it mean to be humble and submit to the Creator-God?

Developing the Proper Relationship

Tozer next points out that "we must of necessity be servant to someone." What does he mean? What is the proof of what or whom we are serving? Tozer indicates that it is the choices we make day after day.

> Our break with the world will be the direct out-come of our changed relation to God. For the world of fallen men does not honor God. Millions call themselves by His name, it is true, and pay some token respect to Him, but a simple test will show how little He is really honored among them. Let the average man be put to the proof on the question of who or what is *above*, and his true position will be exposed. Let him be forced into making a choice between God and money, between God and men, between God and personal ambition, God and self, God and human love, and God will take second place every time. Those other things will be exalted above. However the man may protest, the proof is in the choices he makes day after day throughout his life. (pp. 96–97)

The question arises then: How is a proper Creator-creature relationship developed? By truly exalting and honoring God. Tozer points out: " 'Be thou exalted' is the language of victorious spiritual experience." Read First Samuel 2:30. Think about the lives of Abraham, Jacob, David, others. They did not possess perfection, but rather their "holy intention," their attitudes toward God made the difference.

Whom Do We Honor?

We have to be very careful *whom* we honor! Read John 5:44 and then meditate on the following:

> . . . Christ taught here [John 5:44] the alarming doctrine that the desire for honor among men made belief impossible. Is this sin at the root of righteous unbelief? Could it be that those "intellectual difficulties" which men blame for their inability to believe are but smoke screens to conceal the real cause that lies behind them? Was it this greedy desire for honor from man that made men into Pharisees and Pharisees into Deicides? Is this the secret back of religious self-righteousness and empty worship? I believe it may be. The whole course of the life is upset by failure to put God where He belongs. We exalt ourselves instead of God and the curse follows. (p. 100)

It is important to give God His proper honor. Do not give honor due Him to men. Do not take honor due Him for yourself. One way we can develop this proper relationship with the Creator-God is to praise and exalt Him more. Make such praise a part of your devotional life.

Worship and Praise

As an exercise in praise, read aloud the following passages of Scripture that exalt God: Psalm 57:5–11; Philippians 2:9–11; Psalm 36:5–9; Psalm 33:1–12; Psalm 8:1–9; Psalm 94:1–9; Psalm 104:1–35; Psalm 93; Revelation 5:9–14.

LESSON PLAN—Group Study

AIM: That my students will understand what the Fall did to the Creator-creature relationship. They will also learn what a proper relationship is and how to develop it.

Introduction

1. Open with prayer.

2. Ask the class: What effect did the Fall have on the Creator-creature relationship?

Fallen and Restored Humanity

1. Continue discussing fallen humanity. Read Romans 1:20–32. Discuss what these verses say about the unregenerated person.

2. What restores our relationship with our Creator? Read 2 Corinthians 5:17. Discuss the implications of being new creations in Christ.

A Fixed Center

1. Discuss the importance of a fixed center. Why should God be our center?

2. Read the Tozer quote from pages 94-95 of *The Pursuit of God*.

3. Discuss what Tozer meant by saying that we attempt to "modify" God.

4. Discuss the issue of complete Lordship. Compare and discuss Job 38:1–38 and 40:1–2 with Job 40:3–5 and 42:1–6. Also look at Daniel 4:28–37; James 4:6; Proverbs 16:5; Proverbs 18:12.

5. Discuss the importance of humility and submission in a right relation with God.

Developing the Proper Relationship

1. Discuss what Tozer says is the proof of whom we are serving—our every day choices. Read his quote from pages 96–97 of *The Pursuit of God*.

2. Discuss how a proper Creator-creature relationship is developed.

Whom Do We Honor?

1. Discuss whom we honor. Read John 5:44 and Tozer's quote from page 100 of *The Pursuit of God*.

Worship and Praise

1. If time allows have members of your class read the following Scripture passages that exalt God (you might have them share their favorites as well): Psalm 57:5–11; Philippians 2:9–11; Psalm 36:5–9; Psalm 33:1–12; Psalm 8:1–9; Psalm 94:1–9; Psalm 104:1–35; Psalm 93; Revelation 5:9–14.

Closing

1. Read the prayer at the end of Chapter 8 together.

2. Assign Tozer chapter 9 to read and hand out the study guide questions for next week.

3. Close in prayer.

Session 10

Meekness and Rest

Blessed are the meek: for they shall inherit the earth.
(Matthew 5:5)

W hat do you think it means to be meek? So often we hear that
word and we think wimp or fearful or shy. In the chapter you
have just read, Tozer uses the beatitudes and the Sermon on the
Mount as a backdrop to discussing meekness. Read Matthew chapters 5, 6 and 7. Meditate on the type of persons we ought to be
according to these chapters.

Now compare what Tozer said:

> In the world of men we find nothing approaching
> the virtues of which Jesus spoke in the opening words
> of the famous Sermon on the Mount. Instead of poverty of spirit we find the rankest kind of pride; instead
> of mourners we find pleasure seekers; instead of
> meekness, arrogance; instead of hunger after righteousness we hear men saying, "I am rich and increased with goods and have need of nothing"; instead
> of mercy we find cruelty; instead of purity of heart,
> corrupt imaginings; instead of peacemakers we find
> men quarrelsome and resentful; instead of rejoicing

191

in mistreatment we find them fighting back with every weapon at their command. (*The Pursuit of God*, pp. 103–104)

All our heartaches—and many physical ills—come directly from our sins: pride, arrogance, resentfulness, evil imaginings, malice, greed, etc. Read Matthew 22:37–40. Why do you think Christ said that all other commandments rest on these? If we truly loved our neighbor as ourself what would that eliminate? Study Exodus 20 and see which commandments would not be a problem if we loved our neighbor.

What Is Meekness?

Now go back to meekness and see what Jesus and the Bible said about it. Study the following verses and try to decipher its qualities: Luke 6:29; 1 Peter 2:23; Galatians 5:22–23; 2 Timothy 2:25; Titus 3:2; 1 Peter 3:4. Study these verses to discover some promises: Psalm 37:11, 147:6, 149:9.

Meekness and Rest

Now to tie together both qualities talked about in the chapter, meditate on Matthew 11:28–30. What burden is Tozer talking about?

What is rest? Jesus uses a word in Matthew 11:28 which is translated "heavy-laden" or "burdened" and means a load carried or toil borne to the point of exhaustion. Meditate on the following verses that speak about rest: Exodus 33:14; Psalm 55:6, 116:7. Rest is simply release from that burden. It is not something we do—it is what comes when we cease to do!

Think about the burdens that weigh us down.

1. Pride—the burden of self-love

Why is pride a burden? What does it cause us to do? We will take affront at people who say something about us. We get hurt at the slightest thing. It is tough to have inner peace when we fiercely try to protect ourselves. Remember, God wants to relieve us of the burden of caring what other people say.

But does that mean we should never stand up for ourselves? Does being "meek" mean we are to be doormats? No! As Tozer reminds us:

> The meek man is not a human mouse afflicted with a sense of his own inferiority. Rather, he may be in his moral life as bold as a lion and as strong as Samson; but he has stopped being fooled about himself. He has accepted God's estimate of his own life. He knows he is as weak and helpless as God has declared him to be, but paradoxically, he knows at the same time that he is, in the sight of God, more important than angels. In himself, nothing; in God, everything. That is his motto. He knows well that the world will never see him as God sees him and he has stopped caring. He rests perfectly content to allow God to place His own values. He will be patient to wait for the day when everything will get its own price tag and real worth will come into its own. Then the righteous shall shine forth in the Kingdom of their Father. He is willing to wait for that day. (p. 107)

2. Pretense—the burden of pretending

What does pretense mean? (pretend, make-believe). Pretentious? (showy, pompous, claiming a knowledge we don't have). It is the common human desire to put the best foot forward and hide from the world our real inward poverty. It causes us to think we are better than others. There is an added burden in Christian circles: We put on a spiritual front, often allowing our inner weaknesses to stay hidden.

But what does the Bible say? That we are to come as little children.

3. Artificiality—the burden of hiding

This burden is deadly because we fear that some day we will be careless and someone will be allowed to, as Tozer puts it, "peer into our empty souls."

> Another source of burden is *artificiality*. I am sure that most people live in secret fear that some day they will be careless and by chance an enemy or friend will be allowed to peep into their poor, empty souls. So they are never relaxed. Bright people are tense and alert in fear that they may be trapped into saying something common or stupid. Traveled people are afraid that they may meet some Marco Polo who is able to describe some remote place where they have never been. . . . Artificiality is one curse that will drop away the moment we kneel at Jesus' feet and surrender ourselves to His meekness. (p. 108-109)

How do we get rid of these burdens and accept Christ's rest? We must surrender. We must recognize our complete dependency on Him. Read Second Corinthians 12:9–10. Are you allowing Him to be the strength in your life? Have you surrendered yourself at Jesus' feet?

You may discover a large source of "rest" by meditating on Second Samuel 22:29–37, particularly verses 34–37. Read this passage. The encouragement comes in realizing that while God never promises to keep us from trials, He does promise to supply and equip us for the trials. Verse 34 tells us that God doesn't remove the obstacles, but He does give us the energy to jump over them. Verse 35 tells us that He doesn't keep us out of battle but He does train us for it. Verse 37 tells us that He gives us the sure-footedness we need to walk on any path. What an encouragement to just rest in Him!

Many of us are trying to preserve a comfortable, easy Christianity, when deep down we are suffering from these burdens. But we are too afraid to let them go. We need to turn them over to the Lord, saying: "I recognize my spiritual poverty, my pride and artificiality. God, do a work in my life; I am turning these burdens over to you!" Don't be afraid—just trust. God may shake you up, but He will do the best thing for you!

LESSON PLAN—Group Study

AIM: To cause my students to understand what biblical meekness is and to learn how to rest in God.

Introduction

1. Open with prayer.

2. Read the beatitudes in Matthew 5.

3. Discuss the type of persons we ought to be according to these verses. Compare Tozer's quote from pages 103–104.

4. Read Matthew 22:37–40. Discuss why Christ said all commandments rest on these two. Compare the Ten Commandments (Exodus 20). How is Christ's statement true?

What Is Meekness?

1. Have students read the following verses and point out the qualities of meekness they present: Luke 6:29, 1 Peter 2:23 (non-resistance); Galatians 5:22–23 (fruit of the Spirit); 2 Timothy 2:25, Titus 3:2, 1 Peter 3:4 (gentle, peaceful).

2. Discuss the promises presented in the following verses: Psalm 37:11, 147:6, 149:9.

Meekness and Rest

1. Read Matthew 11:28–30. Discuss the burden Jesus is talking about. (The word Jesus used here means "a load carried or toil borne to the point of exhaustion.")

2. Discuss what is meant by rest.

3. Read and discuss Exodus 33:14; Psalm 55:6, 116:7.

4. Discuss the three burdens Tozer talks about: pride, pretense and artificiality.

5. Discuss the importance of surrendering to Christ's rest. Use 2 Samuel 22:29–37.

Closing

1. Read the prayer at the end of Chapter 9 together.

2. Assign Tozer chapter 10 and hand out the study guide questions for next week.

3. Close in prayer.

Session 11

Tozer Chapter 10

The Sacrament of Living

A sacrament is defined as a "formal, symbolic religious rite, especially the Christian ceremonies of baptism and the Eucharist." Tozer uses the word in his chapter title: "The Sacrament of Living." What does he mean? How can living be a sacrament?

The Sacred and the Secular

One of the greatest hindrances to a Christian's internal peace, according to Tozer, is "the common habit of dividing our lives into two areas—the sacred and the secular." Why is the habit of dividing our lives into sacred and secular such a hindrance to our peace? To answer this question we need to think about the ways in which we divide our lives. The following verses will stimulate your thinking: 1 John 2:15; James 4:4, 1:8; Psalm 73:25. Reread Tozer's words on pages 112-113:

> This tends to divide our total life into two departments. We come unconsciously to recognize two sets of actions. The first are performed with a feeling of satisfaction and a firm assurance that they are pleasing to God. These are the sacred acts and they are usually thought to be prayer, Bible reading, hymn singing, church attendance and such other acts as spring directly from faith. They may be

197

known by the fact that they have no meaning whatever except as faith shows us another world, "an house not made with hands, eternal in the heavens" (2 Corinthians 5:1).

Over against these sacred acts are the secular ones. They include all of the ordinary activities of life which we share with the sons and daughters of Adam: eating, sleeping, working, looking after the needs of the body and performing our dull and prosaic duties here on earth. These we often do reluctantly and with many misgivings, often apologizing to God for what we consider a waste of time and strength. The upshot of this is that we are uneasy most of the time. We go about our common tasks with a feeling of deep frustration, telling ourselves pensively that there's a better day coming when we shall slough off this earthly shell and be bothered no more with the affairs of this world.

This is the old sacred-secular antithesis. Most Christians are caught in its trap. They cannot get a satisfactory adjustment between the claims of the two worlds. They try to walk the tight rope between two kingdoms and they find no peace in either. Their strength is reduced, their outlook confused and their joy taken from them.

I believe this state of affairs to be wholly unnecessary. We have gotten ourselves on the horns of a dilemma, true enough, but the dilemma is not real. It is a creature of misunderstanding. The sacred-secular antithesis has no foundation in the New Testament. Without doubt, a more perfect understanding of Christian truth will deliver us from it.

Walk as Jesus Did

Read First John 2:6. If we are to walk as Jesus did, we must decide what that means. How did Jesus walk? How should He be our model?

Read John 8:28–29. These verses seem to indicate that His whole life was pleasing to the Father. What can we learn from that?

Read First Corinthians 10:31. So that's the answer. But how can we put into practice the command of First Corinthians 10:31? How do we practice living to the glory of God? Read Deuteronomy 10:12 and Matthew 5:16. How does "walking as Jesus did" relate to the following:

- our work?
- our relationships—spouse, children, friends, neighbors, etc.?
- our entertainment?
- our attitudes?

Living to the Glory of God

We must practice "living to the glory of God." That is not always easy. How can we increase our day-to-day awareness of living to the glory of God?

Tozer has a few suggestions:

1. Meditate on this truth each day: "I want to live today for God's glory!"
2. Talk to God often in prayer about this desire. Do this as often throughout the day as you can remember.
3. Try to recall it to mind frequently as you move about your day. Place little reminders ("Live a life to glorify God" written on cards) around—in your car, on your desk, etc.—anywhere you would regularly see them.

Tozer concludes: "Keep reminding God in [your] times of private prayer that [you] mean every act for His glory; then supplement those times by a thousand thought-prayers as [you] go about the job of living. Let us practice the fine art of making every work a priestly ministration. Let us believe that God is in all our simple deeds and learn to find Him there" (pp. 116-117).

Holy Days and Rituals

Next, Tozer talked about the importance to the people of Israel of holy days and rituals. It is important to think about this issue and its purpose. Why did God bring about rituals and holy days in the worship practices of the Israelites? Tozer tells us on page 118 that it was not that God was teaching them that the holiness of things or places was important, but that *God is holy*. A second reason was that God wanted them to learn the difference between holy and unholy!

Tozer also points out that this Old Testament schooling was over when Christ came. What change made these rituals and symbolic days unnecessary? The veil was rent; we now have direct access to the Father. Read Hebrews 10:19–22. Everyone can enter in.

But what does that mean in relation to our worship? How is our worship to be different from that of the Old Testament? Read John 4:21–24 and meditate on its significance to our worship today.

Every Aspect a Holy Act

Making our whole life glorifying to God is not easy. But it is important to our spiritual growth. How does a person make every part of his or her life a holy, uncommon act? Tozer says:

> The motive is everything. Let a man sanctify the Lord God in his heart and he can thereafter do no common act. All he does is good and acceptable to God through Jesus Christ. For such a man, living itself will be sacramental and the whole world a sanctuary. His entire life will be a priestly ministration. As he performs his never-so-simple task, he will hear the voice of the seraphim saying, "Holy, Holy, Holy, is the LORD of hosts: the whole earth is full of his glory." (p. 121)

AIM: To have my students realize that every aspect of their lives should be an act of worship that brings glory to God.

This lesson does not have as many Scripture passages as the other lessons. That means that discussion questions will play a much more vital role than in previous weeks.

Introduction
1. Open with prayer.

2. Discuss what a sacrament is. Why does Tozer title his chapter "The Sacrament of Living"?

The Sacred and the Secular
1. Use the following questions to stimulate discussion. What, according to Tozer, is one of the greatest hindrances to a Christian's internal peace? Why is the habit of dividing our lives into sacred and secular such a hindrance to our peace?

2. Have your students list some ways/areas where we separate the sacred and the secular.

3. Read the following verses and discuss their implications: 1 John 2:15; James 4:4, 1:8; Psalm 73:25.

4. Read the quote from pages 112-113 of *The Pursuit of God*. Discuss.

Walk As Jesus Did
1. Read First John 2:6. Discuss what it means to walk as Jesus did.

2. Read and discuss John 8:28–29.

3. Read First Corinthians 10:31. Discuss how we can practice living to the glory of God. Use Deuteronomy 10:12 and Matthew 5:16 for further discussion. Ask: How does "walking as Jesus did" relate to the following:

- our work?
- our relationships—spouse, children, friends, neighbors, etc.?
- our entertainment?
- our attitudes?

Living to the Glory of God

1. Discuss the concept of "living to the glory of God." How can we increase our day-to-day awareness of living to the glory of God? Use Tozer's suggestions:

A. Meditate on this truth each day: "I want to live today for God's glory!"
B. Talk to God often in prayer about this desire. Do this as often throughout the day as you can remember.
C. Try to recall it to mind frequently as you move about your day. Place little reminders ("Live a life to glorify God" written on cards) around—in your car, on your desk, etc.—anywhere you would regularly see them.

Holy Days and Rituals

1. Discuss the importance of holy days and rituals in the Old Testament. Why did God bring them about?

2. Discuss what changed to make these unnecessary when Christ came. Read Hebrews 10:19–22.

3. Discuss how our worship is to be different from that of Old Testament Hebrews. Read John 4:21–24 and discuss the implications to worship.

4. Discuss: Does this mean we should not celebrate some rituals or special "holy days"? What is good about them? Do they ever become harmful in any way?

Every Aspect a Holy Act

1. Discuss how a person can make every aspect of his or her life a holy, uncommon act. Use the quote from page 121 of *The Pursuit of God*.

Closing

1. Read the prayer at the end of Chapter 10 together.

2. Close with prayer.

Session 12

The Pursuit of God

(This lesson is for the group study only.)

This lesson is designed if you wish to have a review at the end of your study. The aim is simply to discern what impact the lessons have had on your students and to review the main points again.

Class Testimonies

The best review might be to allow students to share with each other what this study has done for them. Asking them to share a significant lesson the Lord taught them, or the most important thing they learned through the study, can be great discussion starters. Allow as much time as you need for this valuable exercise.

Review

Feel free to emphasize the points you feel are most needed. What is provided are simply the major points each chapter made and some statements or related Scriptures about each point.

Chapter 1—Following Hard after God

• God puts within us the impulse to pursue Him. It is our job to do the pursuing.

• You cannot know someone personally and intimately through one visit. Too many Christians stop at their initial finding and have no knowledge of intimacy.
• Philippians 3:4–14.
• Read what Tozer says about complacency on page 17 of *The Pursuit of God*.

Chapter 2—The Blessedness of Possessing Nothing
• We want to hold onto things, relationships, etc. We want to stay in control rather than to recognize that all things are God's.
• Mark 8:34–38; Luke 9:57–62.
• We want a gospel of convenience, but we must give everything to God's control!

Chapter 3—Removing the Veil
• We are created to glorify God. How can we? By walking in truth, maintaining the unity of body, disciplining our bodies, obeying God, keeping pure, doing good deeds before non-Christians, being prepared to suffer.
• Presented the idea that we can enter into God's presence. Hebrews 10:19–23.
• What hinders us? Sin, "self."
• Read Tozer quote from page 43 of *The Pursuit of God*.

Chapter 4—Apprehending God
• There are different levels of belief.
• A true believer knows the reality of God in personal experience.
• The unregenerated person cannot apprehend God; we can.
• 1 Corinthians 2:6–16.
• Faith is the key—Hebrews 11:6.
• We must be "other-worldly." Use quote from page 54 of *The Pursuit of God*.

Chapter 5—The Universal Presence
• God is everywhere; His presence is universal. But the manifestations of that presence are not always readily seen.
• What must we do in order to sense His presence? Use quote from page 60 of *The Pursuit of God*.
• Requires a complete surrender and a life of obedience to His Word.
• We must develop "spiritual receptivity."

Chapter 6—The Speaking Voice
• The aspects of God's spoken and written Word (powerful, purifies, eternal, food, written on our hearts, must love it, it brings light).
• We must be silent to hear. Use quote from pages 75-76 of *The Pursuit of God*.
• We also must act in obedience to God's voice and we must exercise spiritually in order to hear it more often.

Chapter 7—The Gaze of the Soul
• Faith is defined functionally. There is always an action.
• Hebrews 11.
• James 2:14–26. Faith/works: if we truly have faith, the works will be there!
• How do we obtain faith? Ephesians 2:8; Romans 10:17.

Chapter 8—Restoring the Creator-Creature Relation
• Salvation restores the relationship. 2 Corinthians 5:17.
• The only right relation between us and God is full Lordship on His part and complete submission on our part.
• The proof of what or whom we are serving is in our daily choices.
• Only by truly exalting and honoring God is a proper relationship developed.

Chapter 9—Meekness and Rest

• What meekness means—a sense of humility.
• Matthew 11:28–30—the relationship of burdens and rest.
• God wants to relieve us of our burdens: pride, pretense, artificiality.
• We must recognize our complete dependency on Him to experience rest.

Chapter 10—The Sacrament of Living

• Our very life should be an offering of worship to God.
• We need to increase our day-to-day awareness of living to the glory of God.

Conclusion

• How do we know if we have a real relationship with God? The proof is in the fruit we bear. Read John 15:1–17. We all should look back from time to time to see what fruit there is.

INTRODUCTION QUESTIONNAIRE

Please answer these questions honestly. The answers are for your benefit alone.

1. How does one become a Christian?

2. When did I become a Christian?

3. Did becoming a Christian bring any noticeable changes to my life? What were they?

4. Have I ever had a subsequent experience that I would consider to be the filling of the Holy Spirit? When did it happen? What changes did this experience bring in my life?

5. Do I find joy in worshiping God, both privately and with fellow believers?

6. How often do I gather with other believers?
   a. less than weekly
   b. weekly
   c. twice a week
   d. more than twice a week

7. How often do I read my Bible?

    a. never
    b. seldom
    c. once or twice a week
    d. three to five times a week
    e. daily or oftener

8. How often do I converse with God in prayer?

    a. seldom
    b. once or twice a week
    c. three to five times a week
    d. daily
    e. frequently throughout the day

9. When I pray is it a meaningful time of communion, or do I quickly run through a list of requests?

10. When a problem occurs in my life, what is my first response to it?
    a. pray or ask "what is God trying to teach me?"
    b. immediately turn the matter over to God
    c. think "what am I going to do?"
    d. react emotionally
    e. do nothing

11. If I answered c, d or e to question 10, how soon do I get around to a or b?
    a. very quickly
    b. somewhat soon
    c. not very soon
    d. never

STUDY GUIDE QUESTIONS
SESSION 2
Chapter 1: Following Hard after God

1. What does the law of prevenient grace say in practical terms about our seeking God?

2. What is the essence of genuine religion? (John 17:3)

3. Why can't this intimate relationship with God come through our involvement with a body of believers?

4. In what way is the Christian life a paradox?

5. What is deadly to spiritual growth? Why?

6. In what ways does Tozer feel that we need simplicity in our spiritual life?

7. God is speaking to me through this chapter. The one thing I am going to do to develop a closer relationship with Him is:

The steps I am going to take to do this are:

STUDY GUIDE QUESTIONS
SESSION 3

Chapter 2: The Blessedness of Possessing Nothing

1. Tozer had a unique meaning for "poor in spirit." In your own words explain what he feels it means.

2. Read Genesis 22:1–18. While we often look at this passage as Abraham's test of faith, Tozer uses it to stress his point about placing God first in one's life. How does this incident support that point?

3. Why is clinging to things one of the most harmful habits in life?

4. What are some things that are hard for people to give up?

5. What things are hard for me to give up?

6. Read Matthew 19:16–30. What lessons from this passage relate to the theme of the chapter?

7. For further study look at the following passages of Scripture and summarize how each relates to our theme.

Mark 8:34–38:

Luke 12:15–34:

Luke 9:57–62:

Luke 14:26–35:

8. God is speaking to me through this chapter. The one thing I am going to do to develop a closer relationship with Him is:

The steps I am going to take to do this are:

STUDY GUIDE QUESTIONS
SESSION 4
Chapter 3: Removing the Veil

1. For what was mankind chiefly created?

2. In what areas does your life glorify God? In what areas does your life fail to glorify God?

3. What veil has now been removed? What does its removal mean for me as a Christian?

4. According to Tozer, what hinders Christians from entering into the presence of God? In what ways might this hindrance be present in your own life?

Self-love, self-confidence, self-righteousness, egotism

5. God is speaking to me through this chapter. The one thing I am going to do to develop a closer relationship with Him is:

Live for the glory of God — not self. Let Jesus live thru me in me so I am the "vessel" He is the power

The steps I am going to take to do this are:

STUDY GUIDE QUESTIONS
SESSION 5
Chapter 4: Apprehending God

1. "To most people God is an inference, not a reality." Is He a reality to you? If so, explain why and how He is real to you. If not, what could He do to make Himself a reality to you?

2. In what ways can we apprehend God in the same way we can apprehend this world?

3. Why can't unregenerate people apprehend God? (1 Corinthians 2:14; Romans 1:20–21)

4. What is the key for believers to know and have a habitual, conscious communion with God? In other words, what enables our spiritual senses to function? (Hebrews 11:6)

Fantasy assurance of things hoped for
evidence of things unseen

5. What is the difference between imagination and faith?

6. Why do we habitually think of the visible world as real and doubt the reality of the other?

7. What do we have to be if we truly seek to follow Christ?

8. God is speaking to me through this chapter. The one thing I am going to do to develop a closer relationship with Him is:

The steps I am going to take are:

STUDY GUIDE QUESTIONS
SESSION 6
Chapter 5: The Universal Presence

1. Explain in your own words the difference between pantheism and the doctrine of the divine Presence.

SKIP

2. As an exercise of encouragement, rewrite Psalm 139:7–10 in your own words, substituting places and situations (i.e., work, the market, etc.) that are meaningful to you. *How can anyone rephrase something as beautifully written.*

3. Why do some persons "find" God in a way others do not? What is "spiritual receptivity" and what does it have to do with why some have deep experiences and others struggle constantly in the "half-light of imperfect Christian experience"?

4. How does Psalm 27:8 relate to why some people have spiritual receptivity and others do not?

5. What does a person need to do to become more spiritually receptive?

6. God is speaking to me through this chapter. The one thing I am going to do to develop a closer relationship with Him is:

The steps I am going to take are:

STUDY GUIDE QUESTIONS
SESSION 7
Chapter 6: The Speaking Voice

1. What do Psalm 33:6, 9, Hebrews 11:3 and Genesis 1:9 indicate about the power of God's Word?

2. What is the relation of God's spoken Word to His written Word—the Bible?

3. How is God's voice apparent to even the unsaved? (John 1:9–10; Romans 1:20, 2:15)

4. In what ways is God's voice apparent to those who are His children?

5. Has there been a time in your life when you heard His voice? How did you know it was the voice of the Lord?

6. Read Psalm 29. What insights about God's voice can you glean from this passage?

7. How can we develop our sensitivity so we can more clearly and regularly "hear" God's voice?

8. God is speaking to me through this chapter. The one thing I am going to do to develop a closer relationship with Him is:

The steps I am going to take to do this are:

STUDY GUIDE QUESTIONS
SESSION 8
Chapter 7: The Gaze of the Soul

1. Read Hebrews 11:6. In light of this verse and what Tozer says, what do we have if we possess faith?

2. According to Hebrews 11:1, what is faith? Explain it in your own words.

3. What does Tozer mean when he says that faith is defined functionally, not philosophically?

4. How do we obtain faith? (Ephesians 2:8; Romans 10:17)

5. Explain the similarities and differences between the faith of a believer today and that of an Old Testament Israelite.

6. In what ways is faith a virtue that does not regard the self?

7. How does the development of individual faith help the unity of the body of Christ?

8. God is speaking to me through this chapter. The one thing I am going to do to develop my relationship with Him is:

The steps I am going to take are:

STUDY GUIDE QUESTIONS
SESSION 9

Chapter 8: Restoring the Creator-Creature Relation

1. Explain the importance of a "fixed center against which everything else is measured." Why should God be our fixed center?

2. According to Tozer, from where does much of our difficulty as seeking Christians stem? Why does this cause difficulty?

3. What does Tozer mean when he says "we must of necessity be servant to someone"?

4. What results from our truly exalting and honoring God?

5. God is speaking to me through this chapter. The one thing I am going to do to develop my relationship with Him is:

The steps I am going to take to do this are:

STUDY GUIDE QUESTIONS
SESSION 10
Chapter 9: Meekness and Rest

1. According to Tozer, what springs directly from our sins?

2. In Matthew 11:28–30 burden and rest are contrasted. What does each mean in these verses?

3. In what ways does Tozer indicate that one of the causes of our burden is pride?

4. What are the characteristics of a meek person?

5. Explain the other two causes of our burden.

6. God is speaking to me through this chapter. The one thing I am going to do to develop my relationship with Him is:

The steps I am going to take are:

STUDY GUIDE QUESTIONS
SESSION 11
Chapter 10: The Sacrament of Living

1. What, according to Tozer, is one of the greatest hindrances to a Christian's internal peace? Why is it such a hindrance?

2. In what way is Christ our model in overcoming this problem?

3. How can we put into practice the command of First Corinthians 10:31?

4. How do we practice living to the glory of God?

5. What, according to Tozer, was the purpose of the holy days and rituals of the Old Testament? And why does Tozer feel no great emphasis should be placed on such things today?

6. How does a person make every part of his life a holy, uncommon act?

7. God is speaking to me through this chapter. The one thing I am going to do to develop my relationship with Him is:

The steps I am going to take are:

Other titles by A.W. Tozer
published by Christian Publications

For information on these and other titles by Christian Publications, contact us on the web at www.christianpublications.com